GW00986042

THE ISLAND KITCHEN

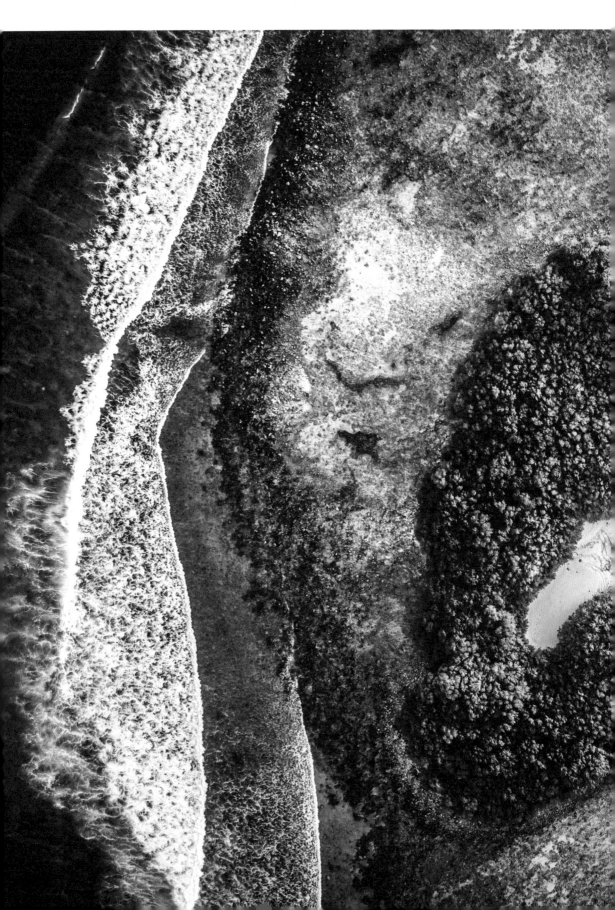

THE
ISLAND
KITCHEN

SELINA PERIAMPILLAI

Photography by Yuki Sugiura
Illustrations by Sarah Greeno

BLOOMSBURY
LONDON · OXFORD · NEW YORK · NEW DELHI · SYDNEY

COMOROS AND MAYOTTE

SEYCHELLES

RODRIGUES

MAURITIUS

RÉUNION

MADAGASCAR

MALDIVES
P.112

INDIAN OCEAN

CONTENTS

0   500   1000

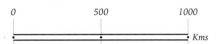

Kms

TASTING THE ISLANDS

The caramel smell of molasses is the scent of Mauritius for me.
It takes me to verdant plantations and the first pressing of sugar cane.
A little waft and I'm suddenly there in the land of my forefathers –
my grandfather laboured in the fields, cutting down those canes.

This multicultural place, with its diverse, utterly glorious food, is my second home. When I am in my kitchen in London I need only to open the door of my larder and for a few moments I am taken back to this majestic part of the world – to the vibrant markets of Port Louis, the capital of Mauritius, as well as the white-sand beaches, dense forests, mountain ranges, waterfalls and spice gardens of the surrounding islands in the Indian Ocean. Rich, dark vanilla pods make me think of Madagascar, where they flourish. Fresh turmeric, coriander and curry leaves, dried cumin and chilli, pepper, cloves, nutmeg and cinnamon transport me to Réunion and Rodrigues, to the Seychelles and the Maldives, to Comoros and Mayotte. All these islands are linked by an invisible thread of flavour, but each of them is quite different. I like to think of them as shiny beads – in various colours and shapes, with their own cultures and style, but together forming a beautiful necklace.

I want you to come with me on a journey to these islands that are in my blood: heavenly places that make my heart and my cooking sing. It's from here that I get my craving for *cari poule*, chicken simmered in thyme, garlic, ginger, masala and fresh coriander leaves; *dhal puri*, soft, thin flatbreads filled with spiced split peas; coriander green chilli chutney and soothing, milky *chai*, just the way Mum makes it, infused with cinnamon bark and split cardamom pods. My parents left Mauritius when they were just beginning their adult lives. They met when they were training to be nurses in England, and were lucky to be introduced by friends from home. They married and made a life in South London, then my older sister and I came along and my dad went on to become a university lecturer. But it was my mum who instilled in me a passion for cooking.

As you might imagine, it's hard for people coming to live in a new, unfamiliar country, and she stuffed her suitcase with spices and the recipes she had scrawled on pieces of paper growing up. As a child, I loved nothing more than to be by her side as she cooked the food from home. And years later, standing next to her in that same kitchen, I realised that together she and I could bring these dishes into other people's kitchens too. This is how I came to have the idea of hosting Mauritian supper clubs in my own home. With the help of my mum, Sabita (or Mama Choo as she would come to be known by our guests), I brought the food of the islands to my table to be shared with strangers, and they loved it.

Many of these recipes belong to my family, with adaptations so that they work in a British home kitchen. Others come from my travels and the food that has thrilled me on my adventures. Creole is the language of many of these islands and when we eat food that's great we say *mari bon*! The literal translation is 'very good', but for me it's also a humble saying that encapsulates the uplifting feeling of togetherness that follows a truly lovely meal that has been shared. The island kitchen is considered the 'heart of the home', and it doesn't matter if the cooking alchemy happens on a stove or on a fire or barbecue, it's the getting together of people, feasting on food, simple or fancy, that is important. This for me is where joy lies, where memories are created, and I hope to share that with you.

Pineapple, coconut, lychees, sweet potatoes, jackfruit, manioc, breadfruit and corn all grow abundantly in the tropical climate of the Indian Ocean islands, and today almost all of these things can also be found in Caribbean, African and Asian shops in the UK. Indeed, most of the ingredients I use in my recipes are reasonably easy to find – I've had to form my creations around what is available to me at home. British-grown sweetcorn comes into its own late in summer, a time that I relish because it reminds me of our annual Mauritius holiday, when my dad would get a roasting *karai* (a cast-iron pan that looks a bit like a wok), lay it over open flames on the hot sand, and we would watch as the kernels frantically started popping. He'd boil bright-yellow husks to be eaten fresh with butter and spices,

curry them with potatoes, or grind them to make *chapatis*. Apart from the sand, I can do all of this at home – and so can you.

In my years of travelling across the Indian Ocean islands, each with their different landscape, people and scale – Madagascar is vast, Rodrigues is tiny – one of the things that I have come to love about them all is that knives and forks are not commonly used. Of course, they are in the finest restaurants and hotels, but not in real homes outside of that bubble. Local people eat with their hands, grabbing handfuls of rice and using that as a vessel with which to scoop up curry, or taking flaky, hot, bubbly flatbread and folding it around a *cari*, all of which brings a greater connection to the texture and feeling of the food. This enjoyment in experiencing a meal is at the heart of 'island time', where the day is relaxed and dinner becomes sensual because you're using your fingers to bring flavours together. Here the rhythm is slow and, as you explore the recipes in this book, you might find yourself stepping down a pace, embracing island time in your kitchen like I do. You may be far from the sea and the salty air, it may be winter and the sun might not be on your face, but these dishes can carry your senses and, of course, your imagination away.

There's a mélange of styles across this archipelago, influenced by the people that arrived on these shores: sailors and colonisers, traders and settlers, coming with their own cuisines and flavours. There's such incredible diversity, so every dish tells a story of its own. But there is commonality too. For me it's the vibrant markets, shouty and alive, where you can barter for the freshest produce. And on every island one of my favourite things is the sight of the singular fisherman, out on a little boat with his line. They may seem lonely out there on their own, but when they come back to shore they often huddle for shade together under

a tree, their catch laid out on a table – snapper, sea bream, mahi mahi, perhaps – and when I see a group of these hard-working guys I run up and buy what I can, propelled by a desire to get a sweet, sticky marinade made and the grill lit.

Each of these islands has many amazing dishes. Here I've chosen the ones that thrill me, that take me to another place when I'm in the midst of the long, dark nights of winter and I want to bring sunshine to my plate. But most importantly, these are recipes that people cook at home in these faraway places without a huge amount of effort, so you can too. You'll find simple, light, summery recipes alongside hearty, robust stews and curries. There are spicy chutneys and tangy pickles to accompany all manner of dishes, local street foods that are perfect snacks and indulgent desserts full of tropical fruits and laced with a healthy dose of rum.

I'm not a trained chef. I cook in a small kitchen (I'm not kidding you). Over the years I've followed recipes and I've cooked from instinct. I've learned from my mother and other members of my family, from home cooks as well as chefs on the islands. They've taught me about flavour, tradition and pleasure. They've shown me how spices work together to create harmony, and that delicious chutneys bring balance to a dish. I've learned that rolling out flatbreads can be truly meditative and that seeing them bubbling on a flat pan or over a naked flame can be thrilling. They've given me a treasure: the knowledge that the true essence of the island kitchen can come to any home. I know that you can bring it to yours too. Chuck out all those old spices, buy some fresh bags of cinnamon and cumin and all the rest, breathe them in and let's begin our island journey.

THE INDIAN
OCEAN KITCHEN

Across the Indian Ocean islands gorgeous fruits and vegetables, heady spices, aromatic herbs and punchy chillies flourish, providing the building blocks for a vibrant, uplifting cuisine. I'd like to introduce you to the ingredients that play a starring role in the dishes you'll find there, and in the recipes that follow.

VEGETABLES

BREADFRUIT This starchy vegetable varies in size, but can grow up to the size of a cannonball. It has a potato-like texture and is covered in a green prickly skin; its hard outer layer is peeled with a sharp knife and the flesh inside chopped into chunks or sliced. It is commonly made into mash with coconut milk, fried like chips (p.155) or fritters, baked in banana leaves or simply boiled until tender with a smear of butter and served as a side dish.

CASSAVA (MANIOC) The cassava root is an integral part of Creole cuisine and is popular throughout the tropics, where it is used much like the potato. Its rather unpromising appearance belies its versatility: beneath its brown, bark-like exterior is a white flesh that can be used to make the Mauritian stew *kat kat*, soup, pancakes, glutinous cakes or biscuits.

To peel a cassava Start by trimming off the ends of the cassava root with a sharp knife, then chop the root into two or three large chunks. Stand each piece on end and use a sharp knife to cut away the skin in large pieces. Quarter each piece lengthways; the woody core can then be taken out before the white flesh is used for cooking.

CHOU CHOU This pear-shaped fruit, which is eaten as a vegetable, goes by many names, including christophine (France and the Caribbean), choko (Australasia) and chayote (America). It is found in almost all markets on the Indian Ocean islands and is often served in gratins like my Pumpkin & chou chou gratin (p.120) or added to salads or braised-style dishes (*touffés*) with onions, garlic, ginger and thyme. Here in the UK you can find it in most Asian or Chinese grocers.

To peel a chou chou Wear disposable gloves or peel the chou chou under running cold water because it releases a white sap that can be quite sticky on the hands. (A trick of my mum's is to smear her hands in a little oil.) Hold the chou chou in one hand and, using a vegetable peeler or sharp knife, peel the skin off, rotating as you go. Chop the white flesh into pieces and remove the seeded core with a knife.

OKRA Also known as 'ladies' fingers', these vibrant green pods, filled with tiny, white edible seeds, are ridged along their length and slightly fuzzy. The flavour is subtle, so okra works best when bold spices and herbs are added to them. They can be eaten raw, or lightly steamed, in fresh salads, such as the Okra & tomato salad with red onion (p.106), or sautéed with garlic and ginger, but it's crucial not to overcook them or they can become slimy. When choosing okra look for a bright green exterior and avoid any that are bruised or dull in colour. Store okra in a paper bag in the fridge for up to 3 days.

SQUASH AND PUMPKIN Pâtisson (yellow squash) or patty pan as they are called in Mauritius, come in a wonderful array of shapes and sizes. They can be stuffed with a meat filling, added to curries, stir-fried with mustard seeds, chilli and ginger or made into a sweet-savoury chutney. The Réunion way is to turn them into a divine gratin covered in bubbling cheese and béchamel sauce (p.120). Pumpkin is seasonal, but for most recipes you should be able to find alternatives such as butternut squash or sweet potato.

SWEET POTATO This has been one of the staple foods of the islands for centuries and now the Seychelles cultivates up to five different varieties of this sweet and starchy root crop, which can be boiled, grilled, steamed, puréed or baked. Two of my favourite ways to use it are in the Creamy sweet potato soup (p.116), zingy with lime, and in the unctuous, aromatic dessert Sweet potato with nutmeg & cinnamon (p.207). Sweet potatoes should be stored loose (not wrapped in plastic) in a cool, dark and well-ventilated place, where they will keep for up to 10 days.

TARO AND CRESSON LEAVES These leafy greens are widely used around the islands, and particularly in the famous Mauritian dish *brede songe*. The leaves of the taro can be stewed or stir-fried with garlic, ginger and onions. When making *bouillon* (soup), the watercress (*cresson*) is gently warmed through with the residual heat, as in the Watercress & pak choi broth (p.115). Spinach, kale or Swiss chard work well as substitutes.

FRUITS

BANANA Banana trees line the riverbanks and wetlands of the islands; *banane zinzli*, or 'dwarf bananas', are an especially flavourful variety. When they are not eaten straight off the branch, they are cooked in tarts, sponge cakes or fritters (p.203 and p.208). Plantains are used as an alternative, while green (unripe) bananas are primarily cooked in curries with dried shrimp.

COCONUT As coconuts grow in abundance across the region it's no surprise that both the delicate milk and silky flesh of the coconut are used in curries, spice mixes, marinades, chutneys, salads and desserts. I always have a tin of coconut milk or a block of coconut cream to hand in the kitchen as it can immediately transform a dish into something wonderfully fragrant. Coconut milk is more liquid in consistency, whereas the cream is thicker and hard and needs to melt gently while cooking. Fresh coconut can be grated to make a delicious zingy chutney (p.189).

To crack a coconut Locate the three 'eyes' and gently pierce with a pointy, sharp knife or skewer (one of the eyes is normally easier to pierce than the others). Hold over a bowl or glass to catch the coconut water and drink! Then wrap the coconut in a tea towel, hold in one hand and tap with the back of a cleaver or hammer (be careful!)

in the same place until it cracks open. Separate the white flesh from the shell with a spoon or knife and peel as much of the brown hard skin off as you can. Grate using a food processor or hand grater and it is ready to use.

MANGO In Réunion they grow a number of varieties of mango: 'Carotte', 'Heidi', 'American' and 'José' to name a few. These orange-hued, succulent fruits can be devoured as they are but they also work wonderfully with other ingredients, such as in the Toasted coconut, mango & carrot salad (p.110) or pickled in their unripe state with mustard seeds, fenugreek, dried chillies and turmeric – not to mention in fragrant desserts, such as the Mango & lime tarte tatin (p.218). To test for ripeness, gently squeeze the fruit; if it yields slightly it should be ready to eat.

To prepare a mango Holding the mango firmly, place it on its side on a chopping board and use a sharp knife to slice off the 'cheeks' (just to one side of the large stone). Use a spoon to scoop out the flesh or score into cubes or slices (cutting through until your knife reaches the skin). Bend the skin backwards to cut off all the pieces. Holding the stone, peel the remaining skin off and cut the flesh into cubes or slices (or eat it right off the stone).

PAPAYA On the islands papaya or paw paw is used raw or 'green', grated into sour salads and spiked with chillies or added to meat dishes early on in cooking – the enzymes in papaya are called papain and help to tenderise and break down meat fibres, resulting in a softer texture. You can find these green, hard-skinned fruits in Asian or Chinese markets; ripe papayas can easily be found in supermarkets. These are great cut into wedges for a refreshing fruit salad garnished with mint.

PINEAPPLE The pineapples in Mauritius are the small, sweet 'Victoria' pineapples – these are often hand-carved and pickled with red chilli and salt or made into a refreshing salad with tamarind (p.105). Their natural sweetness means they are also used in desserts and cakes, blended into boozy rum cocktails or eaten warm and caramelised as a dessert (p.222). Try to find the ripest fruits; if it smells sweet like pineapple juice it is probably ripe inside – the leaves should also pop out with a slight tug.

To prepare a pineapple Use a sharp knife to slice the top and bottom off the pineapple. Stand it upright and carefully make thin slices down all the sides until you have removed most of the prickly skin, leaving as much flesh as possible. Use a smaller knife to remove the 'eyes' or brown spots (I make v-shaped trenches diagonally with my knife to cut them out). Stand the pineapple up again, slice in half, and then into quarters. Slice off the hard core from each wedge and the flesh is ready to be chopped into chunks or slices.

WATERMELON The key thing with watermelon, one of my favourite summer fruits, is to chill it in the fridge before you eat it. You can also blend it into a refreshing juice with coconut and lime (p.238), a drink that is typically chosen in the Maldives to break the Ramadan fast. When buying a watermelon look at its underside or belly and find its 'field spot' – a yellowish area that indicates whether it is ripe inside. It should sound hollow when you tap it.

OPPOSITE: PREPARING A COCONUT

OVERLEAF: CUTTING A MANGO AND A PINEAPPLE

HERBS & SPICES

CARDAMOM Both black cardamom (strong and smoky) and green cardamom (sweet and subtle) feature in cooking across the islands, but green cardamom is more commonly used. The pods contain tiny seeds of aromatic warmth and are used, once crushed and the husks removed, to add a depth of flavour to rich curries. They can be found in most supermarkets, so keep a jar of cardamom pods on hand to flavour curries and rice dishes, and desserts like Cardamom chocolate mousse with pistachios (p.229). I tend to drop a pod or two into my tea to give it an aromatic dimension.

To prepare cardamom Gently crush the pods in a pestle and mortar to release the seeds. Discard the husks, then pound the seeds into a fine powder.

CHILLI A central ingredient in Indian Ocean cooking, chillies can be found in enormous mounds in the local markets of the region. They come in a dazzling array of varieties, from the extremely hot 'Githeyo mirus' chilli from the Maldives to the small green 'Bullet' chillies from Mauritius. Each island has its own distinctive version of chilli paste: in Rodrigues they use lemon to create a zesty, fiery chilli mixture (p.197), while in Madagascar a hot chilli dipping sauce is made with plenty of red chillies, vinegar and oil (p.196).

The chillies I use in most of my recipes are long, green, thin 'finger' chillies or small red Thai-style chillies, and these can be found in the large supermarkets and Asian grocers. Some specialist online stores (p.256) sell a wide range of chillies, from mild to extremely hot. Where possible I have suggested alternatives to achieve similar levels of spiciness, and in some cases the more readily available chilli paste or powder can be substituted if you can't get hold of fresh chillies.

To prepare chillies Use disposable gloves when preparing really hot chillies; this will prevent them getting in your eyes or stinging your hands. Using a sharp knife, slice the top off the chilli where the small stalk is, then slice in half lengthways and scrape out the white membrane and seeds (this is the hottest part of the chilli), although if you like the heat (I do!), keep them in. Slice lengthways into thin shreds or finely chop, and do make sure you wash your hands thoroughly afterwards.

CINNAMON Once traded as currency and cultivated in the Seychelles, Mauritius and Madagascar, cinnamon bark is peeled off the tree and laid in the sun to dry; it is then either rolled into cinnamon sticks or ground into powder. It is used to add depth to meat curries and is often paired with vanilla for sweet treats and desserts.

CLOVES These dried flower buds of the clove tree are grown across the islands. They can be used sparingly, either whole or ground, to impart a strong, sweet but slightly peppery note to dishes. Cloves go well in spiced meat dishes, like my Slow-cooked duck with cinnamon & cloves (p.40), and are a key component in many spice masala blends. You can also substitute with a little ground allspice.

CORIANDER Also known as cilantro or Chinese parsley, this is one of my favourite herbs. All parts of the plant are edible, but the fresh leaves and the dried seeds are those most traditionally used. In Mauritius fresh coriander is blitzed into a spicy chutney (see Coriander green chilli chutney, p.190) but it is mostly used as an aromatic garnish.

CUMIN With a rich, pungent aroma, this warm and slightly bitter spice is delicious in curries and forms the base of numerous spice mixes. I always have a jar of cumin seeds and ground cumin in my store cupboard. Lightly toasting cumin seeds in a dry pan releases their aroma – they can then be added to dishes to give a little extra bite and flavour or they can be ground to a fine powder.

CURRY LEAVES These are shiny, dark green, aromatic leaves – and are not related to curry powder at all. They are used to add flavour and depth to curries and have a unique lemony-herb flavour that is released when the leaves are bruised or crushed slightly and fried in oil. You can buy them fresh from Asian grocers or dried in supermarkets.

CURRY POWDER There are probably as many theories as to the origin of the word 'curry' as there are variations on the blend of spices used. You can easily find pre-made blends in the supermarkets, which come mild, medium or hot, but if you have time there's nothing more rewarding than blending your own combination; the key ingredients are usually cloves, cumin, coriander, fenugreek, cinnamon, cardamom, turmeric and chillies. Dry-toast the spices slightly to release their oils and aromas and then blitz to a powder in a spice grinder. In my recipes for Traditional-style beef cari, Fragrant goat cooked in masala spices and Lonumirus spiced fried fish (p.44, p.48 and p.152), each has its own distinctive island spice mix.

GARLIC Highly valued throughout the ages as a culinary spice, garlic is one of the oldest cultivated plants in the world and is much used in Asian cooking. It goes hand in hand with ginger to create the base of a *rougaille* (see Sausages in spicy tomato sauce, p.54).

GINGER Fresh ginger has a peppery flavour, with a sweet hint of lemon, and the aroma is pungent and sharp. It's widely available in supermarkets; go for plump, unblemished roots.

To prepare ginger To peel ginger, use the side of a small teaspoon to scrape away at the skin. Then simply grate, slice or cut the ginger into batons.

MUSTARD Mustard seeds can be white, yellow, black or brown; the lighter coloured seeds tend to be much milder than darker ones, which are exceedingly pungent, so it's important to use these sparingly. When fried for a few seconds, the flavour of mustard seeds becomes nutty and aromatic. Across the islands mustard seeds are commonly used in pickles (see my Green bean, cabbage & carrot mustard pickle, p.186). They are also often paired with fish, as in my Mustard- & turmeric-marinated tuna (p.82).

NUTMEG Pierre Poivre was the first citizen to introduce (or smuggle!) spice plants to Mauritius and Réunion in the 1760s, nutmeg and cloves being the main ones. The brown seed can be grated on a fine grater or it can be bought in powder form. This fragrant spice brings a little kick of warmth and curious complexity to desserts like Sweet potato with nutmeg & cinnamon (p.207).

PEPPERCORNS Pink and black peppercorns add vibrant pops of colour and underlying heat to desserts as well as savoury dishes. You can find black peppercorns in all supermarkets, while the rarer pink peppercorn is sourced from Réunion or Madagascar; see p.256 for online suppliers or look in specialist shops.

TAMARIND The pods from the tamarind tree contain a sticky pulp that is used to add a sour note to curries like my King prawns with tamarind & coconut (p.98), as well as to salads and chutneys (p.105 and p.189). It comes fresh in pods, in a jar as a concentrated paste (you may find this in large supermarkets) and in blocks of pressed tamarind pulp, which are very useful if you can't get hold of fresh pods.

To prepare tamarind Tamarind paste can be used just as it is. If you are using whole pods, crack the shells and remove the seeds and pulp. Soak in a bowl of hot water for 15–20 minutes, then use your fingers to squeeze them and separate the fleshy pulp from the seeds. Strain the tamarind, discarding the liquid and pushing the pulp through a fine sieve into a bowl, discarding the fibres, seeds and membranes. If you are using a block of pressed tamarind, simply break off a piece and soak and strain as above. The tamarind pulp can be used straight away or frozen in batches to use later.

THYME This unlikely but popular herb is used in Mauritian and the surrounding islands' cooking thanks to its French ancestry. These small green-grey leaves add a sweet, earthy hint to *rougailles* (p.54) and sautéed Creole vegetable dishes. Lemon thyme is sometimes used to add a more citrus tang, which works in subtle desserts. You can find fresh thyme in the supermarket, or keep a pot on your kitchen windowsill to use as and when. I always have a jar of dried thyme as well; if you can't find any, herbes de Provence or oregano would suffice.

TURMERIC Also known as curcuma, turmeric is cultivated in the tropics and has been used in India for millennia, not just as a spice but for medicinal purposes. The root looks very similar to fresh ginger, but has a deep golden-orange colour and is most often used in powder form. With an earthy yet subtle taste, this spice adds a bright yellow natural colouring to dishes and is found in many traditional curry powder mixes. It is used extensively in poultry, lamb, fish, vegetable, lentil or rice dishes – my mum adds it to milk for a warm, comforting drink.

VANILLA The vanilla grown in Madagascar is plump, with a glossy dark-brown skin and packed with black seeds. Each vanilla orchid blossoms for only a few hours and must be individually pollinated by hand. The bean only gains its fragrance after it is fermented, and is odour-free at the time of harvest. The complex pollinating process makes vanilla the second most expensive spice in the world (after saffron). It is frequently used to flavour desserts and black tea, in spiced rum (*rhum arrangé*) or infused into sugar.

To prepare vanilla Slit the pod open lengthways with a sharp knife, then scrape out the small seeds using the tip of the knife. Unused vanilla pods should be stored in an airtight container in a dark, cool place.

PULSES & GRAINS

LENTILS Réunion is famous for some of the best lentils in the world, namely the soft brown lentils that are cultivated in mountainous Cilaos. They are cooked in recipes like Creamy lentils with thyme & turmeric (p.124). Other types include red split lentils, and yellow split peas which are used to make the popular snack Chilli dhal fritters (p.156) and the robust, comforting dish Lamb soup with lentils & cracked wheat (p.50). Most supermarkets stock a range of dried pulses, from yellow split peas to red lentils and brown lentils, great for thickening soups and stews, while green and puy lentil varieties can be found tinned for quick cooking or adding to salads. I always wash dried lentils thoroughly to remove any impurities. This was a job my mum always gave to me when I was younger – I'd pretend I was searching for gold!

RICE Originally brought over from Indonesia and Malaysia, this important grain is eaten every day on the islands

– often more than once a day; in fact Madagascar has a saying, 'You will only be satisfied if you eat enough rice.' Rice is eaten for breakfast as porridge, as the main event combined with meat and vegetables and as a staple side dish. It is even turned into the refreshing drink *ranovola*, which is made by toasting cooked rice in a pan until nutty and slightly burnt, and then steeping in hot water, straining and serving chilled.

To prepare rice Rice is best soaked or washed thoroughly in cold water before cooking to remove some of the starch, giving a fluffier result. As a rule of thumb, with white basmati rice I always use one part rice to two parts water. Bring up to the boil, then turn down to a simmer and cook for 6–8 minutes (until most of the water has evaporated), then cover and steam for a few minutes more. Fluff up with a fork to separate the grains. Timings will vary with brown rice, pudding rice and other varieties, so do check the packet instructions before cooking.

USING THIS BOOK

Essential to island-style eating is taking your time, sitting down with loved ones and enjoying the experience of eating together. It's traditional to have several dishes around the table, including rice, grilled fish, soups and rich curries, and there are always condiments of some sort, from spicy pickles to fresh chutneys and fiery chillies. Served alongside are plenty of warm *rotis* (flatbreads), which are torn into shards before being used to scoop up sauce from curries.

I have included a menu planning section, which you will find on pp.245–248, to help guide you if you want to create a whole menu from a particular island, a barbecue-style feast or a special meal suitable for vegans and vegetarians.

- All eggs are medium unless otherwise stated.

- I don't often deseed my chillies as I like the extra kick. However, feel free to scrape them out if you still want the underlying heat in your dish, but without blowing your socks off.

- Dishes are seasoned to taste or finished with flaky sea salt and freshly ground black pepper.

- Fresh curry leaves are a secret ingredient that is really worth seeking out. If you can't find them in your local Asian supermarket try some online suppliers (p.256). Leftover leaves can be stored in the freezer or fridge, but they will naturally dry out and lose a bit of flavour. Dried curry leaves (available from large supermarkets) can still be used if you can't find any fresh.

- When it comes to spices, I tend to buy whole spices in small amounts and grind them myself. The flavour is much more pronounced this way – ready-ground spices lose their flavour over time. It also really does make a difference to dry-toast whole spices before grinding to release their aromas, while similarly whole spices often need to be sizzled in hot oil to release their aromas in cooking. Any leftover dry spice mixes can be stored in airtight jars, while wet pastes will keep in the fridge for a few days.

- I have a basic stocked kitchen, but one special pan I use is called a *tawa* or flat crêpe pan. They can be found in good cook shops and online and make the job of cooking and flipping *rotis* and *chapatis* so much easier; if you don't have one a shallow non-stick frying pan will do the job. A spice grinder or pestle and mortar and a blender are also useful to whip up spice mixes, chutneys and juices.

MEAT

Sticky Chicken with Garlic & Ginger
AKOHO MISY SAKAMALAO, MADAGASCAR

Sunny-side-up Egg, Chicken & Pak Choi Rice Bowl
BOL RENVERSÉ, MAURITIUS

Coconut Chicken
AKOHO SY VOANIO, MADAGASCAR

Chicken in Yoghurt & Saffron Sauce
KALIA DE POULET, MAURITIUS

Chicken Wings with Tomatoes
MBAWA YA TOMATI, COMOROS & MAYOTTE

Slow-cooked Duck with Cinnamon & Cloves
SALMI DE CANARD, MAURITIUS

Beef & Pork Stew with Spring Greens
ROMAZAVA, MADAGASCAR

Traditional-style Beef Cari
CARI BOEUF, MAURITIUS

Rice Stew with Leafy Greens & Beef
VARY AMIN'ANANA, MADAGASCAR

Fragrant Goat Cooked in Masala Spices
CABRI MASSALÉ, RÉUNION

Lamb Soup with Lentils & Cracked Wheat
HALEEM, MAURITIUS

Sausages in Spicy Tomato Sauce
ROUGAILLE SAUCISSE, RÉUNION

Four-spice Pork Kebabs with Peppers
BROCHETTES DE PORC, RÉUNION

Grilled Spiced Lamb Chops with Lemon
MAURITIUS

Pork Loin Glazed with Honey & Thyme
RODRIGUES

MEAT

COOKING MEAT DISHES on the Indian Ocean islands rarely involves conventional ovens; instead rich, slow-cooked beef *cari*, deep with fragrant Mauritian masala and scents of sweet cinnamon, is simmered gently for hours on the stove until it melts in your mouth, while the French-inspired Sausages in spicy tomato sauce (p.54) from Réunion, a smoky, vibrant, ruby-red tomato and sausage stew layered with chilli, thyme, garlic and onion, is cooked in a deep clay pot over an outdoor wood fire. In summer, meat is marinated overnight in sticky honey and dark, salty soy sauce and then skewered with vegetables, ready for charring on the grill or barbecue – the people of these islands love their alfresco cooking. In cooler seasons, locals opt for semi-dry curries like *salmi* (p.40), duck infused with rich red wine and warm spiced cloves, or the robust and wholesome *haleem* (p.50), a Muslim dish famed for its tender lamb pieces flaked into a sea of the most comforting amalgamation of lentils and cracked wheat.

In home kitchens, as well as the more familiar chicken, beef, pork and lamb, you will also find dishes using wild boar, venison, goat, rabbit – even hedgehog. Although beef, goat and buffalo meat are sometimes imported from Australia or South Africa, hunting for small game on the islands is a tradition that continues today. I still remember my uncle returning home carrying large hares over his shoulder, which he would then meticulously prepare for *civet de lièvre*, a dish cooked with white wine, thyme, chillies and garden peas.

Elaborate meat dishes are usually reserved for special occasions such as weddings, New Year and religious festivals, which are almost always centred around a communal feast. In our family these food rituals involve bringing out large pots of goat *cari*, buttery ghee-laced biryanis and a plethora of pickles and freshly made chutneys to create a truly memorable meal. However, the recipes that follow are for every moment worth celebrating, whether you are cooking a feast for family and friends or just looking for something rich and comforting to perk you up after a long day. Although I've drawn inspiration from traditional dishes that are cooked in home kitchens across the islands, they ultimately all share the same principle: flavourful meats with vibrant leafy greens, vegetables or pulses, which resonate with an exquisite combination of Indian Ocean spices.

The secret to this recipe is the marinade that infuses the chicken with the vibrant tastes of ginger, garlic, salt and tangy lemon zest. The chicken is cooked together with slices of onion and sweet strips of pepper that mix with the gloriously sticky juices in the pan. Serve with Hot chilli dipping sauce (p.196) and a generous spoonful of steamed rice or Creole saffran rice (p.131).

STICKY CHICKEN WITH GARLIC & GINGER
AKOHO MISY SAKAMALAO, MADAGASCAR

8 chicken thighs, skin on, bone in
½ tsp sea salt
Zest of 1 lemon
5cm piece of fresh root ginger, peeled and grated

6 garlic cloves, finely chopped
2 tbsp coconut oil
1 large onion, finely sliced
1 red or yellow pepper, finely sliced
Freshly ground black pepper

SERVES:
4
PREP:
15 MINS, PLUS OVERNIGHT MARINATING
COOK:
1 HOUR

· Using a sharp knife, make two or three diagonal slashes into the skin of each chicken thigh and place in a large bowl. Add the salt, lemon zest, ginger and garlic. Rub the ingredients well into the chicken thighs, making sure to wash your hands afterwards. Cover the bowl with cling film and place in the fridge overnight to marinate.

· The next day, heat the coconut oil in a large, wide frying pan over a medium heat. Add in the marinated chicken thighs (they should all fit snugly into a single layer in the pan) and brown nicely on both sides, which can take up to 10–15 minutes. Season with pepper.

· Remove the chicken from the pan, add in the sliced onion and sauté until softened, around 5–7 minutes. Carefully tip away all but 2 tablespoons of the fat, return the chicken to the pan, skin side up, and add in the red or yellow pepper. Cover and cook over a low heat for 20 minutes until nearly cooked throughout, turning the chicken thighs over halfway through and stirring the onion.

· Remove the lid and increase the heat to medium-high. Leave to bubble away for 7–10 minutes, until the juices have reduced, the chicken skin is charred and glossy and the onions are sticky and caramelised. Serve on rice and spoon some of the sticky chicken juices from the pan over the dish, with a dollop of chilli sauce on the side if you wish.

The Creole 'bol renversé' translates (unsurprisingly) as 'upside-down bowl'. It's a theatrical Sino-Mauritian dish that is found on Chinese restaurant menus and in cafés dotted across the island.

The surprise is in the unveiling of the perfect dome of rice, topped with chicken and vegetables in a soy and oyster sauce. It is then crowned with a fried egg, which I take great pleasure in piercing so the golden yolk trickles down the sides. You can eat this with a teaspoon of Green chilli paste with lemon (p.197) or the Ripe tomato salad with chilli & lemon (p.109).

SUNNY-SIDE-UP EGG, CHICKEN & PAK CHOI RICE BOWL
BOL RENVERSÉ, MAURITIUS

250g basmati rice
2 tbsp vegetable oil
1 onion, finely chopped
2 garlic cloves, finely chopped
2.5cm piece of fresh root ginger, peeled and finely chopped
1 carrot, cut into thin matchsticks
125g shiitake mushrooms, sliced
130g baby corn, chopped
300g chicken breast, cut into strips, then halved

200g pak choi, trimmed, stalks cut diagonally into thin slices, leaves torn
2 tbsp light soy sauce
1 tbsp oyster sauce
1 tsp fish sauce
1 tsp cornflour, mixed with 150ml water
1 tbsp olive oil
4 eggs
3 tbsp finely chopped chives

SERVES:
4
PREP:
20 MINS, PLUS 30 MINS SOAKING
COOK:
15 MINS

• Firstly soak the rice for 30 minutes in cold water (or wash a few times until the water runs clear). Drain well. Cook your basmati rice according to the packet instructions.

• Place all your prepared vegetables and the chicken on a large plate, so everything is ready to add to the wok.

• Place a large wok over a high heat and add the vegetable oil. Once the oil is hot add in your onion, garlic and ginger and, using a metal spoon or spatula, keep stirring the ingredients in the pan to avoid burning. Fry for 1–2 minutes.

- Tip in the carrot, mushrooms, corn and chicken strips, give that all a good mix together and cook for 2 minutes while stirring. Next goes in the pak choi, which will wilt down eventually. I use all of it, even the white harder ends, which retain a nice crunch when cooked.

- Create the base of the sauce by adding the soy, oyster and fish sauces into the wok and give them a good stir. Pour in the cornflour water mixture – this will thicken it all up and result in a glossy, light brown liquid.

- Turn the heat down to a medium simmer, cover and gently cook for 10 minutes until the chicken is cooked throughout and the corn and carrots are softened, but still retain a slight crunch. Set aside.

- In the meantime, fry the eggs. Heat the olive oil in a frying pan on a medium-high heat and crack in the eggs, one at a time. Cook for around 4 minutes, taking care not to break the yolks, then turn off the heat and let them sit for 1 minute.

- Take four medium-sized bowls, one per person, and begin to layer up your magic bowl. First divide the chicken and vegetable mixture into each bowl, then divide the rice equally and gently press down so you can't see any of the chicken mixture.

- Take a dinner plate and get ready to invert your bowl (this is the trick). Place the plate over your bowl and, holding the plate securely, flip it over (so the bowl is upside down on your plate). Gently lift up the bowl to unveil your *bol renversé*, and carefully place an egg on the top. Scatter with chives and add chilli paste on the side.

Pictured overleaf

This is a popular Christmas meal in Madagascar, prepared with tender pieces of chicken nestled in a creamy, pinkish sauce made from coconut milk and ripe tomatoes. There is a light hint of spice from the cayenne pepper that tingles the back of your throat, but it's not too spicy. Serve over rice and accompany with some steamed fresh greens.

COCONUT CHICKEN
AKOHO SY VOANIO,
MADAGASCAR

600g chicken thigh fillets,
  skinned, cut into halves
Juice of ½ lemon
2 tbsp vegetable oil
1 red onion, finely sliced
2 garlic cloves, finely chopped
2.5cm piece of fresh root ginger,
  peeled and finely chopped

2 ripe tomatoes, chopped
½ tsp cayenne pepper
400ml tin coconut milk
Sea salt and freshly ground
  black pepper
1 tbsp coriander leaves, to garnish

SERVES:
4
PREP:
15 MINS,
PLUS
30 MINS
MARINATING
COOK:
40 MINS

- First marinate the chicken in a bowl with the lemon juice and some salt and pepper. Cover with cling film and leave in the fridge for 30 minutes.

- In a deep saucepan or a large, deep frying pan over a medium heat, add the vegetable oil and sauté the onion with the garlic and ginger for 5–7 minutes until softened, stirring occasionally.

- Add in the chopped tomatoes, cayenne pepper and the chicken and give it a good mix together. Let this cook for 5 minutes while stirring to get a golden colour on the chicken. Pour in the coconut milk and turn down to a low simmer. Cook uncovered for around 25 minutes until the chicken is cooked throughout. Check for seasoning, scatter with coriander and serve immediately with rice and greens on the side.

This Bengali-inspired dish is normally served for the Muslim festival Eid in Mauritius, but is also cooked at home for family occasions. The recipe uses myriad spices, similar to those in a biryani, and is rich with aromas, creaminess from the yoghurt and golden tones from the saffron. Serve with rice, a side salad like the Ripe tomato salad with chilli & lemon (p.109) or simply a spoonful of Sweet mango & red chilli chutney (p.194).

CHICKEN IN YOGHURT & SAFFRON SAUCE
KALIA DE POULET, MAURITIUS

8 chicken thighs, skinned, bone in
7–8 tbsp vegetable oil or ghee
2 large onions, sliced
2 medium potatoes (500g),
    peeled and cut into 2cm cubes
Small pinch of saffron strands
2 tomatoes (200g), roughly chopped
Sea salt and freshly ground
    black pepper
1 small bunch of mint or coriander,
    leaves picked and chopped,
    to garnish

For the marinade:
1 onion, roughly chopped
5 garlic cloves

2cm piece of fresh root ginger,
    peeled and chopped
Small handful of mint leaves
Small handful of coriander leaves
150g natural yoghurt
2–3 green chillies
1 tsp salt

For the ground spice mix:
2 tbsp ground cumin
2 tbsp garam masala
6 cardamom pods, seeds only, crushed
    or ¼ tsp ground cardamom
1 tsp ground cinnamon
½ tsp ground cloves
½ tsp ground nutmeg

SERVES:
4
PREP:
20 MINS,
PLUS
OVERNIGHT
MARINATING
COOK:
1 HOUR

· Place all the marinade ingredients in a blender with about 2 tablespoons water and whiz to a smooth, pale green paste. Pour the marinade over the chicken pieces in a bowl, add in the ground spice mix and stir to ensure all the chicken is coated. Cover with cling film and refrigerate overnight.

· Before cooking, take the chicken out of the fridge to bring it to room temperature.

· Next make the fried onions and potatoes. In a large frying pan, heat up 5–6 tablespoons of the vegetable oil or ghee (enough to cover the base of the pan) to a medium-high heat. When hot, tip in the onion and fry for 7–10 minutes, stirring to ensure an even colour, until crisp, charred and golden brown. Drain on a plate lined with kitchen paper.

· Using the same pan as the onions (there should be enough residual oil in the pan), fry the potato cubes until golden brown on all sides; this takes around 7–10 minutes. Drain on a plate lined with kitchen paper.

- Soak the saffron strands in 100ml hot water for 5 minutes.

- Place a large saucepan or a large, deep frying pan with a lid over a medium heat with the remaining 2 tablespoons of vegetable oil. Once hot, add all of the chicken plus the marinade into the pan. Give this a good stir and cook for 3–5 minutes, until the chicken begins to sizzle. Tip in the tomatoes and saffron, including the water it was soaking in. Combine everything together, cover and cook for 20 minutes, stirring occasionally.

- Tip in the half-cooked potato cubes, cover again and cook for around another 20 minutes until the chicken is cooked throughout and the potatoes are tender. The sauce may look like it has split slightly as the oil rises to the top, but this is fine. Check for seasoning and adjust accordingly.

- Serve immediately over basmati rice, scattered with those lovely charred fried onions and fresh mint or coriander leaves.

These sticky chicken wings are irresistibly good. On the islands, street-side vendors grill them over charcoal, but at home they can be made in a saucepan. I have added smoked paprika to give them an extra hint of smokiness, and although palm oil is traditionally used, here groundnut oil bestows an underlying nutty tone. The combination of paprika and tomatoes gives these chicken wings a lovely crimson-red finish. Pile them onto a platter to share or serve on individual mounds of rice.

CHICKEN WINGS WITH TOMATOES

MBAWA YA TOMATI, COMOROS & MAYOTTE

2 tbsp groundnut oil
1 onion, chopped
1 tsp smoked paprika
1kg chicken wings
½ tsp sea salt
½ tsp freshly ground black pepper

1 tsp ground cumin
400g tin chopped tomatoes
1 tsp tomato purée
Pinch of caster sugar
1 spring onion, sliced diagonally,
   to garnish

SERVES:
4
PREP:
10 MINS
COOK:
55 MINS

- Preheat a large saucepan over a medium-high heat, drizzle in the groundnut oil and add the chopped onion and paprika. Stir frequently for around 5 minutes and fry until softened and reddish in colour.

- Add the chicken wings, salt and pepper and sprinkle in the cumin. Fry the wings in the spices for 3 minutes, turning over halfway until the skin is browned on both sides and covered in those aromatic spices.

- Pour in the chopped tomatoes, tomato purée, sugar and 250ml cold water and give it a good stir so it's all mixed well together. Bring to a boil, then reduce the heat to medium and cook, uncovered, for 45 minutes. Once the chicken is cooked through, the sauce will have reduced to a rich tomato coating on the wings. Serve garnished with spring onions over white basmati rice or simply get your hands dirty and enjoy as they are.

MAURITIUS

MAURITIUS IS KNOWN for its white-sand beaches fringed with coral reefs lying under turquoise seas. But it's also a gourmet paradise, with a magical mélange of flavours. The food is the story of the people who migrated to the island – which lies at the confluence of Asia, Europe and Africa's maritime routes – over the centuries. It is a cuisine that came from native Africans forced here as slaves, French colonisers who ruled in the eighteenth century, the Chinese who travelled from Guangzhou in the 1780s and Guangdong in the nineteenth century, and Indians who arrived as indentured labourers and whose descendants now make up over half of the population. Our penchant for afternoon tea lies with the British, who took over in 1810.

When the Portuguese discovered Mauritius in 1507, calling it and its neighbours Rodrigues and Réunion the 'Ilhas Mascarenhas' (the Mascarene Islands) – named after the explorer Pedro Mascarenhas who first set foot there – there were no indigenous people and therefore no native cuisine. The dodo, our endemic flightless bird, now extinct, was still thriving.

The mish mash of people who landed around the 330km of coastline meant that Creole (also known as 'Creole Morisyen', which came about as French colonisers tried to communicate with the slaves forced here from Africa) became the language of the island. The influx of cultures brought manifold types of dish together on the Mauritian table: from India came *cari* (curry); from France, *rougailles* (light stews) scented with thyme, *bouillon* (soup), *daube* and *coq au vin* – as well as fabulous pastries and tarts; from China, rice, noodles and dumplings, and the wonderful *gateau zingli*, sesame balls made from sweet potato, glutinous rice or sometimes red bean paste, deep fried until slightly chewy inside and crisp outside, then flecked with sesame seeds.

The food of Mauritius comes alive in the place locals call the Grand Bazaar, in the middle of Port Louis' Central Market. Stalls are stacked with just-picked fruit and vegetables in a kaleidoscope of colours. You'll see: huddles of yellow dwarf bananas; blushing pink lychees just plucked from the trees, their leaves still attached; deep green and red chillies of all shapes and sizes; and piles of chou chou, prickly breadfruit and baby pineapples (the sweetest I've ever tasted). Stall-holders cook over little burners and charcoal grills. Soft brown *roti* cooked on a *tawa* are smeared with butterbean curry, coriander chutney and chilli before being curled into a *papier cornet* and wrapped in pages of an old telephone directory. One bite and I'm in heaven, truly back in the land of my parents, my second home.

● *Port Louis*

MAURITIUS

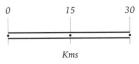

0   15   30

Kms

The 'salmi' (pronounced 'sal-me') is a French method of cooking, where duck is roasted or slow-cooked in a rich red wine sauce. This Mauritian version has a Creole flair, with a hint of chilli, soy sauce and coriander to finish. Give the duck time to marinate overnight in the cloves, cinnamon, red wine and garlic and, when cooked, it will be aromatic and fall off the bone. Serve with rice and sautéed vegetables on the side.

SLOW-COOKED DUCK WITH CINNAMON & CLOVES
SALMI DE CANARD, MAURITIUS

2 duck legs, skin on
300ml red wine
2 tbsp vegetable oil
1 onion, finely chopped
2 garlic cloves, finely chopped
2cm piece of fresh root ginger, peeled and finely grated
1 tbsp thyme leaves
2 ripe tomatoes (200g), diced
200ml vegetable stock
1 tbsp soft light brown sugar
1 tbsp chopped coriander
1 tbsp chopped parsley

Sea salt and freshly ground black pepper

For the 'salmi' paste:
½ cinnamon stick or 1 tsp ground cinnamon
8 cloves
2 garlic cloves, finely chopped
2 red chillies, deseeded and finely chopped
1 tbsp vegetable oil
1 tbsp dark soy sauce

SERVES:
2
PREP:
25 MINS, PLUS 2 HOURS OR OVERNIGHT MARINATING
COOK:
2 HOURS

· First make the *salmi* paste. In a small frying pan over a high heat, toast the cinnamon and cloves for 30 seconds until the fragrance rises up from the pan. Put the toasted spices into a spice grinder or use a pestle and mortar to pound to a powder. Add the garlic cloves and red chillies and continue pounding until you have a coarse paste. Mix in the vegetable oil and soy sauce until thoroughly combined.

· Take the duck legs and, using a sharp knife, score the skin a couple of times so the marinade can permeate through.

· Place the duck legs in a large freezer bag or mixing bowl, rub the paste into them and then add in 100ml of the red wine. Tie the bag securely and place in the fridge overnight or for a couple of hours if you don't have time.

· The next day, add the oil to a flameproof casserole dish over a medium-high heat. Take the duck legs out of the marinade and pat dry with kitchen

paper. Discard the marinade. Place the legs in the casserole dish and fry on both sides until golden brown, around 5 minutes per side. Remove the legs and set aside.

- Reduce to a medium heat, add in the onion, garlic and ginger and cook for 5 minutes to sweat these off. Next, add in the thyme leaves and tomatoes. Give this a good stir. Add in the remaining 200ml of red wine to deglaze the pan and leave to bubble away until reduced by two-thirds. Pour in the stock and add the sugar.

- Return the duck legs to the casserole dish, cover the dish and simmer over a low heat for 1 hour. Uncover and continue to cook for another 30 minutes until the duck legs are tender and the meat falls off when forked. Season with salt and pepper, then scatter with fresh coriander and parsley. Serve with sautéed vegetables and rice.

'Romazava' is a national dish of Madagascar: a hearty stew with juicy pieces of meat that gently fall apart on first bite, in a warming tomato–beef broth. This dish traditionally uses 'zebu' (cattle grazed in Madagascar) alongside pork and sometimes chicken, with mustard greens and rocket leaves for their peppery notes. I've used beef and pork, which melt perfectly into the stew, with spinach, rocket leaves and seasonal spring greens. Tumble a large spoonful of the stew over white rice with Hot chilli dipping sauce (p.196) on the side.

BEEF & PORK STEW WITH SPRING GREENS

ROMAZAVA, MADAGASCAR

500g beef chuck, cut into 2cm pieces
3 tbsp vegetable oil
2 onions, diced
5 garlic cloves, finely chopped
5cm piece of fresh root ginger, peeled and finely chopped
1–2 'Serrano' chillies, deseeded and finely chopped (can be substituted with 'Habanero' or 'Jalapeño' chillies or 1 tsp cayenne pepper)

6 ripe tomatoes (500g), roughly chopped
300ml beef stock
500g pork belly slices, 2cm thick
50g spinach
50g spring greens or kale
50g rocket
Sea salt and freshly ground black pepper

SERVES:
6
PREP:
20 MINS
COOK:
2 HOURS
45 MINS

· Bring the beef chunks to room temperature and season with salt and pepper.

· In a large flameproof casserole dish over a high heat, add in 2 tablespoons of the oil and sear the beef pieces, in batches, until browned all over, around 3–5 minutes per batch. Remove with a slotted spoon onto a plate. Reduce the temperature to medium, add the diced onion to the same pan and fry until translucent, around 5–7 minutes, scraping the bottom of the pan.

· Put the beef back into the pan with the onion and add in the garlic, ginger, chillies and tomatoes and stir well. Tip in the stock, bring up to a boil and then turn down to a gentle simmer. Cover and cook for 1 hour 15 minutes.

· Towards the end of the cooking time, add the remaining oil to a large frying pan. Season the pork belly and sear on all sides over a high heat until it is slightly caramelised and lightly browned, around 5–7 minutes. Remove, cool slightly and cut into 2cm pieces. Add to the casserole dish with the beef, give it all a gentle stir and cover again. Cook for a further 30 minutes, then remove the lid so it's slightly ajar and cook for 30 minutes to reduce the sauce. Stir occasionally so it doesn't stick at the bottom.

· Once the cooking time is up, tip in the greens and cook for another 10 minutes. Check the meat is cooked through and is soft and tender. Taste for seasoning and adjust. Serve over steamed basmati rice.

'Cari' is the Mauritian Creole word for 'curry', but it differs from the Indian dish due to its unique blend of Provençale herbs combined with fiery chilli and aromatic spices, such as cinnamon. This makes for a delicate, scented sauce, intensified by the rich beef juices from the pan. The curry tastes even better if you make it the night before, allowing the flavours to steep.

In Mauritius we make a goat, lamb or beef 'cari' for special occasions such as New Year, when a big pot is shared amongst close family and neighbours, a meal over which there is much storytelling and laughter. Freshly cooked 'rotis' (p.138) are served for scooping up the glossy 'cari' sauce, along with a spicy chutney, such as Fresh coconut, mint & tamarind chutney (p.189).

TRADITIONAL-STYLE BEEF CARI
CARI BOEUF, MAURITIUS

5 tbsp vegetable oil
500g beef chuck, cut into 2cm pieces
1 large onion, finely chopped
3 garlic cloves, finely chopped
2.5cm piece of fresh root ginger,
   peeled and finely chopped
3 thyme sprigs, leaves picked
3–4 green chillies, finely chopped
1 cinnamon stick
1 tbsp finely chopped coriander stalks,
   plus 2 tbsp coriander leaves
400g tin plum tomatoes
2 tsp salt
1 bunch of spring onions,
   finely chopped

For the Mauritian curry powder:
6 tbsp coriander seeds
6 tbsp cumin seeds
1 tsp fenugreek seeds
   or ground fenugreek
1 tsp fennel seeds
1 tsp ground cinnamon
2 tsp ground turmeric
10 curry leaves
2 dried Kashmiri red chillies
   or any dried red chilli

SERVES:
4
PREP:
25 MINS
COOK:
2 HOURS
20 MINS

- Start by making the Mauritian curry powder. In a bowl, mix all the spices together. Take a large frying pan, place over a medium-high heat, tip in the spice mix and gently toast the spices for 30 seconds until aromatic (do not let them burn). Grind the spices in an electric spice grinder or use a pestle and mortar to pulverise into a fine powder. If any large pieces remain, tip the curry powder through a sieve. Store in an airtight jar and keep in a cool, dry place.

- For the beef *cari*, place a large flameproof casserole dish on a high heat, add 2 tablespoons of the oil and sear the beef chuck in batches for 5 minutes to caramelise and brown. Remove from the dish and set aside.

xt add in the remaining 3 tablespoons of oil, turn down to a medium-
h heat, throw in the onion, garlic and ginger and stir. Sweat for
minutes until softened, taking care not to burn the garlic and ginger
t lower the heat if they brown too quickly). Add in the thyme, chilli
cinnamon stick.

small bowl mix 4 tablespoons of the Mauritian curry powder (see note
w) with a splash of water, stirring to create a wet paste.

r the paste into the onion and mix well until the onion is all tinged
w. Add in the coriander stalks, reserving the leaves for later, and tip
ne beef chuck, stirring occasionally to ensure the meat is combined
well with all those spices.

- Pour in the plum tomatoes, breaking them up in the pan, then add 100ml
  water. This should come up to just below the level of the meat in the pan.
  Cover and simmer over a low heat for 2 hours, stirring halfway through to
  ensure nothing is sticking to the bottom of the pan. Leave the lid slightly
  ajar for the last 30 minutes of cooking to thicken and reduce the sauce.

- Add in the salt and stir, then taste for seasoning and add more salt
  and pepper if needed. Check the meat is tender and soft. Discard the
  cinnamon stick.

- Scatter over the spring onion and fresh coriander leaves. Serve the *cari*
  alongside rice or *rotis* and chutney.

Note

- If you make your own Mauritian curry powder (you will have some left
  over as it makes around 85g/14 tablespoons) it can be stored in a jar and
  used another time to make a *cari* with chicken, fish or vegetables using the
  same method (though they will cook more quickly). However, you can
  substitute it with mild curry powder found in supermarkets.

In Madagascar they call green leafy vegetables 'bredes', and use everything from the leaves and shoots to the stems. This warming one-pot recipe is a hearty and verdant dish, which can be packed full of all manner of seasonal greens: here I've used spinach, kale and watercress.

RICE STEW WITH LEAFY GREENS & BEEF

VARY AMIN'ANANA, MADAGASCAR

2 tbsp vegetable oil
1 onion, finely diced
2 garlic cloves, finely chopped
2.5cm piece of fresh root ginger, peeled and finely chopped
500g minced beef
1 tsp sea salt
½ tsp freshly ground black pepper

2 tomatoes (200g), roughly chopped
50g spinach, chopped
50g watercress, chopped
50g kale or collard greens
150g white rice, washed in cold water and drained

SERVES:
4–6
PREP:
20 MINS
COOK:
40 MINS

- In a large, deep saucepan, heat the oil over a medium heat, add in the onion and sauté for 5–7 minutes until softened. Tip in the chopped garlic and ginger and mix well with the onion, cooking for a further 2 minutes.

- Add in the minced beef with the salt and pepper and, using a spoon, break up any lumps. Cook the meat for around 5–7 minutes until it is nicely browned. Scatter in the tomatoes and all of the spinach, watercress and kale – they will probably reach the top of the pot but will wilt down slowly. Let this cook for 3 minutes until most of the greens have wilted, then pour in 400ml water.

- Add the washed rice to the pot, give it a gentle stir, bring to the boil, then cover with a lid. Reduce the heat to medium-low and simmer for 15–20 minutes. After that time the rice should be cooked and the liquid absorbed.

- Serve a heaped spoonful on a plate with a dollop of Hot chilli dipping sauce (p.196) on the side.

This classic dish from Réunion has its roots in Indian cuisine, and is commonly prepared for Tamil New Year and other celebrations. What's special about it is the unifying spice blend of 'garam massalé' that flavours the 'cari', and many Réunionese families have their own secret recipe! I met a local chef on the island, Pierre, who after a little persuasion divulged his grandmother's magic combination. The 'cabri massalé' has a glossy, chocolate-coloured finish that coats the tender goat meat, which is served with rice and a tomato salad (p.109).

Source goat meat online and at your butcher, or use mutton or spring lamb as a substitute.

FRAGRANT GOAT COOKED IN MASALA SPICES
CABRI MASSALÉ, RÉUNION

750g goat meat, cut into 3cm pieces (ask your butcher to do this – it's ok if you have some bone in there as it will add extra flavour)
1 tsp sea salt
½ tsp freshly ground black pepper
4 tbsp vegetable oil
1 large onion, finely chopped
5 garlic cloves, finely chopped
2 spring onions, finely chopped

For the 'garam massalé':
4 tbsp coriander seeds
2 tbsp fenugreek seeds
10 cloves
10 curry leaves
2 tbsp cumin seeds
2 tsp yellow mustard seeds
1 tsp ground nutmeg
1 tsp ground cinnamon

SERVES:
4
PREP:
20 MINS
COOK:
2 HOURS
40 MINS

· First make the *garam massalé*. In a small frying pan over a high heat, toast all the spices together for 30 seconds or so until aromatic.

· Tip the spices into a grinder or blender and whiz to create your spice mix. Decant into an airtight jar. The mix can be kept in a cool dry place and used for making other dishes (as this makes more than you need).

· Season your goat meat with the salt and black pepper, and mix well.

· In a deep flameproof casserole dish, add in the oil over a high heat. When the oil is hot, add the goat meat in batches and sear, turning over for 3–5 minutes using a spoon or tongs. Remove with a slotted spoon and set aside.

- Reduce the heat to medium and tip in the onion and garlic. Stir for 5 minutes to loosen those gnarly bits at the bottom of the dish – lots of flavour here! Sprinkle 3 tablespoons of the *garam massalé* over the onions and coat them in these glorious aromatic spices.

- Add the meat back to the dish and top up with 400ml water or until the pieces are just covered. Turn the heat down to low and simmer, covered, for 2 hours. Stir the meat halfway through cooking. Then take off the lid and cook for another 30 minutes or until tender; the sauce will reduce and thicken until it just coats the meat.

- Season with salt and pepper and scatter over the spring onion before serving. Eat with rice and a tomato salad.

Originating from the Middle East and India, the 'haleem' – a type of thick, hearty soup – is all about slow cooking. Flaked nuggets of lamb, wheat and lentils are enrobed in a broth of robust spices. I always sear the meat before cooking so it gains a flavourful browned crust, and if I have ghee (clarified butter, found in Asian supermarkets), I add a teaspoon into the oil when frying the onions to give them a buttery taste (though you can do perfectly well without). Serve with basmati rice or baguette.

LAMB SOUP WITH LENTILS & CRACKED WHEAT
HALEEM, MAURITIUS

Vegetable oil, for frying,
   plus 1 tsp ghee (optional)
2 onions, finely sliced
500g lamb shoulder/leg, cut into
   3cm pieces (ask your butcher to
   do this) or substitute with stewing
   lamb (approx. 20 pieces)
4 garlic cloves, finely chopped
1 tbsp finely chopped fresh root ginger
2 shallots, finely sliced
1 tsp ground turmeric
1 tsp ground cinnamon
½ tsp ground cardamom or
   16 cardamom pods, seeds only,
   ground
1½ tsp ground cumin

1 tsp chilli powder
50g yellow split peas,
   rinsed and drained
50g bulgur wheat or pearl barley,
   rinsed and drained
50g brown lentils, rinsed and drained
½ tsp salt
Small handful of mint leaves,
   finely chopped
Small handful of coriander leaves,
   finely chopped

To serve:
Natural yoghurt
2 spring onions, finely chopped
1 lemon, cut into wedges

SERVES:
4
PREP:
10 MINS
COOK:
2 HOURS
10 MINS

• In a large frying pan over a medium-high heat, add a good glug of vegetable oil (and 1 teaspoon ghee if you have it) to cover the bottom of the pan. Once hot, tip in all the sliced onions and fry until you have crisp browned onions, charred on the edges. This is will take around 7–10 minutes. Drain on a plate lined with kitchen paper and set aside.

- In a large flameproof casserole dish or deep saucepan, add in 3 tablespoons of the vegetable oil over a high heat and brown the meat in two batches, 5 minutes per batch, until the lamb is a caramelised golden-brown colour and seared all over. Remove from the pan and set aside. Add in another 1 tablespoon oil, then the garlic, ginger and shallots and sweat for 5–7 minutes, stirring occasionally. Tip in the seared lamb pieces and combine with the garlic and ginger.

- Place the spices – turmeric, cinnamon, cardamom, cumin and chilli powder – in a small bowl and mix well with a spoon. Add in a splash of water (2 or 3 tablespoons) and mix to a wet paste. Spoon this into the pan with the lamb, ensuring all the pieces are coated.

- Next add in the split peas, wheat and brown lentils, 600ml water and the salt. Bring to the boil and then turn down to a low simmer. Cover the pan and cook for 1 hour 30 minutes. Halfway through cooking, gently stir to prevent it sticking on the bottom of the pan. If you would like a thinner consistency, you can add in more water 30 minutes before the end of the cooking time.

- Scatter in the mint and coriander and cook for another 10 minutes. Check the lamb is tender and breaking apart and the lentils are cooked.

- Swirl a spoonful of yoghurt into the *haleem*, top with the spring onion and crispy onions, and serve with rice or with a buttered crust of French baguette. Squeeze over lemon wedges as you eat.

Pictured overleaf

I first had the pleasure of trying this dish in Cilaos, a small village surrounded by forested mountains in the centre of Réunion. At a small, home-style eatery I met owner Aliette, who made a traditional 'rougaille', a spicy tomato sauce made from ripe tomatoes, chillies and thyme, and cooked with smoked sausages. It is reminiscent of a French cassoulet, but spicier! The taste was exceptional, with deep, earthy notes – and a touch of Creole flavour from the smoked paprika and turmeric. Serve spooned over white rice.

SAUSAGES IN SPICY TOMATO SAUCE
ROUGAILLE SAUCISSE, RÉUNION

6 smoked or herb sausages
2.5cm piece of fresh root ginger, peeled and finely chopped
4 garlic cloves, finely chopped
2 red chillies, finely sliced (add more if preferred)
1 tsp sea salt
3 tbsp olive oil

1 large onion, finely chopped
4 thyme sprigs, leaves picked
½ tsp ground turmeric
½ tsp smoked paprika
6 ripe tomatoes (600g), roughly chopped
Pinch of caster sugar
1 spring onion, finely sliced

SERVES:
4
PREP:
20 MINS
COOK:
50 MINS

· Fill a deep saucepan halfway with water and bring it to the boil. Gently drop in the sausages whole and boil for 10 minutes.

· Using a pestle and mortar, pound the ginger, garlic, chillies and salt to a paste for 3–4 minutes until combined well. Set aside.

· Drain the sausages and pat dry with kitchen paper, place on a chopping board and allow to cool slightly. Cut each sausage into three or four pieces.

· In a large frying pan over a medium heat, add 1 tablespoon of the oil and fry the sausage pieces for 4–5 minutes until slightly browned all over, turning frequently. Take out the sausages and set aside.

· In the same pan, add the remaining 2 tablespoons of oil over a medium heat. Tip in the onion and sweat for 5–7 minutes, then spoon in the ginger, garlic and chilli paste made earlier and stir well. Add the thyme, turmeric and paprika and stir into the onion until coated. Cook for 2 minutes.

· Tip in the tomatoes and combine with all the other ingredients. Add 100ml water and the sugar. Bring to a boil, then turn down to a simmer and cook slowly for 15 minutes until the sauce has reduced and thickened. Add the sausages back into the pan to cook for a further 10 minutes. Taste for seasoning, scatter with spring onion and serve with rice.

RÉUNION

WITH MOUNTAINS AND gorges, waterfalls, blue lagoons and one of the world's most active volcanoes, Piton de la Fournaise, Réunion is the middle sister of sibling islands known as the Mascarenes. Lying to the east of Madagascar and southwest of Mauritius, some of the palm-fringed beaches here may not be as white and sandy as elsewhere in the Indian Ocean, but the coral reefs are largely intact, the seas here are not overfished and the catch is bountiful: a seafood lover's paradise.

Early in the morning, when the boats have returned, you'll see gobsmackingly fresh red tuna, swordfish, Patagonian toothfish and rock lobsters being sold along the seafront. The Réunionese will study these coastal specimens with sharp eyes and a keen nose. Once satisfied, they'll pay and take their purchases home because almost everyone loves to cook (locals seldom eat out). If it's a Sunday, every family will be off to a *pique nique* – a Creole institution where everyone gathers outdoors to share grilled meat and fish, cooking *caris* (curries) over wood fires, along with *rougaille* (a spicy sauce of tomatoes, onion and chilli) and rice.

It's the blended nature of the Réunionese (three-quarters of the population are *métis*, people of mixed origin) that makes a visit here an eye opener for any food lover – it's very Creole and at the same time very French, with wonderful notes of Chinese, African, Indian and Tamil. *Cari* is the most popular dish, using chicken, fish, wild duck and

even *tenrec*, a local hedgehog. Flavours on Réunion are punchy: ginger, herbs and spices all play their part, along with *quatre-épices* (allspice leaves that combine hints of bay, pepper, cinnamon and cloves), turmeric, curry leaves, ginger and chilli – I love the tiny, fiery local variety known as 'Piment-oiseau'. Every family makes their own Réunionese *garam massalé* (garam masala paste) with a 'secret' mix of ground coriander, cumin, cloves, cinnamon and nutmeg.

The Portuguese landed in Réunion in around 1507, but it was not until twenty Frenchmen and forty-two Malagasy slaves created a settlement in 1649 that the island became inhabited. Coffee was the first crop to be planted, then sugar cane, lentils and even some vineyards. Once called Île Bourbon, it is a French overseas department. In the capital, Saint-Denis, you'll find bistros and boulangeries in streets that have a tropical yet Parisian feel.

Réunion became the world's first producer of cultivated vanilla because of the brilliance of a twelve-year-old slave, Edmond Albius, who, in 1841, developed a technique for hand-pollinating vanilla orchids that would allow them to be harvested away from their native Mexico. The island also produces the tiny Victoria pineapple, and fifty varieties of mango. Both of these fruits are often served with a salt and chilli mixture which brings a souring heat to the sweetness – perfect.

Saint-Denis

RÉUNION

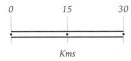

0   15   30

Kms

On the lively seafront markets on the west coast of Réunion, you can spot from afar the smoke billowing off large barbecue grill pans lined with sizzling brochettes (kebabs or grilled meats). The festive smell of cloves, nutmeg, cinnamon and ginger, combined with the marinated pork in its caramelised sticky soy and honey glaze, never fails to draw in crowds of people.

When making these at home on the barbecue for friends, I marinate the pork overnight to get that punchy flavour. Once cooked they are great to grab and eat straight off the barbecue or skewered into a mound of rice.

FOUR-SPICE PORK KEBABS WITH PEPPERS
BROCHETTES DE PORC, RÉUNION

500g pork loin, shoulder or neck,
    cut into 4cm chunks
1 large red pepper, cut into chunks
3 tomatoes, deseeded and cut into
    chunks
1 large red onion, cut into chunks
1 tbsp olive oil
Sea salt and freshly ground
    black pepper

For the marinade:
2 garlic cloves, roughly chopped
2cm piece of fresh root ginger,
    peeled and finely chopped
3 tbsp light soy sauce
½ tsp ground cinnamon
½ tsp ground cloves
½ tsp ground nutmeg
Pinch of cayenne pepper
1 tbsp runny honey

12 wooden skewers, soaked in water
    for 30 minutes

SERVES:
4
(12 SKEWERS)
PREP:
30 MINS,
PLUS
2 HOURS
OR
OVERNIGHT
MARINATING
COOK:
15 MINS

- First make the marinade. Using a pestle and mortar, pound the garlic and ginger to a paste, then add in the soy sauce, cinnamon, cloves, nutmeg, cayenne pepper and honey. Combine using a spoon.

- Place the pork in a mixing bowl with the marinade and rub well into the meat. Cover and refrigerate to marinate for at least 2 hours, or ideally overnight.

- Place the pepper, tomato and red onion in a bowl and drizzle with the olive oil to coat the vegetables.

- Start to assemble the brochette skewers: first take a piece of pork and pierce in the middle and push down to the end of the skewer, then alternate the tomato, peppers, onion and pork until all the skewers are full. Season with salt and pepper and brush with the remaining marinade juices.

- Place the skewers on a preheated grill or barbecue for around 5 minutes on each side until the pork is cooked throughout but still juicy and tender. Serve over steamed white rice.

These are perfect for the barbecue or grill, accompanied by an ice-cold Mauritian Phoenix beer. The lamb chops are scented with lemony herbs and have a slight underlying sweetness of honey and cinnamon, which is great with lamb. You can prepare this ahead by marinating the meat overnight so the flavours have a chance to penetrate. To finish, dip into yoghurt with finely chopped mint leaves and squeeze over extra lime or lemon. This goes well with my Tamarind pineapple chilli salt salad (p.105) or the Toasted coconut, mango & carrot salad (p.110).

GRILLED SPICED LAMB CHOPS WITH LEMON
MAURITIUS

6 lamb chops
2 tbsp olive oil
Sea salt and freshly ground
  black pepper

For the marinade:
2 tbsp dark soy sauce
2 tsp runny honey
½ tsp ground cloves
2 tsp ground cinnamon

1–2 red chillies, finely chopped
4 thyme sprigs, leaves picked
2 tsp grated fresh root ginger
2 garlic cloves, finely chopped
Zest and juice of 1 lemon

To serve:
1 lemon or lime, cut into wedges
Natural yoghurt
Finely chopped mint leaves

SERVES:
2
PREP:
25 MINS,
PLUS
2 HOURS
OR
OVERNIGHT
MARINATING
COOK:
UNDER
10 MINS

· Place all the marinade ingredients in a large mixing bowl and mix well. Turn the lamb chops in the marinade until coated all over. Cover in cling film and refrigerate for at least 2 hours or overnight.

· Take the lamb chops out 30 minutes before cooking to come to room temperature. Brush with the olive oil.

· Heat a grill pan over a medium-high heat until almost smoking (this can also be done on the barbecue). Add the lamb chops and sear for 2 minutes on the first side before flipping over and cooking on the other side for 3 minutes for medium rare or 3½ minutes for medium. Take out and rest on a plate covered with foil for 5 minutes before serving with lemon (or lime) wedges, a dollop of yoghurt mixed with the mint leaves and some basmati rice.

Eucalyptus honey is a local speciality in Rodrigues; it has a mellow, woody aftertaste and a beautiful amber colour. Here it makes a delicious, sticky glaze for the pork, enhanced with flecks of fresh thyme and tangy lime. You can buy eucalyptus honey in some supermarkets, but if you can't find it, any golden honey is fine. Serve with comforting sides like Mum's spicy mashed potato (p.127) or Pumpkin & chou chou gratin (p.120).

PORK LOIN GLAZED WITH HONEY & THYME
RODRIGUES

1.5–2kg piece of rolled and tied pork loin, with the skin scored
2 garlic cloves, finely sliced
4 thyme sprigs, leaves picked
1 large onion, roughly sliced
1 tbsp sea salt
500ml chicken stock
1 tbsp plain flour
Freshly ground black pepper

For the glaze:
2 tsp ground cinnamon
2 tbsp honey, ideally eucalyptus
Juice of 1 lime
1 tbsp vegetable oil

SERVES:
4–6
PREP:
15 MINS
COOK:
2 HOURS, PLUS 20 MINS RESTING

· Take the pork out of the fridge 30 minutes before cooking to bring up to room temperature. Make the glaze by mixing the cinnamon, honey, lime and oil in a small bowl.

· Preheat the oven to 230°C/Fan 210°C/Gas 8.

· Turn the pork rind-side down and, with a small knife, make about six deep incisions along the meat. Poke a sliver of garlic and a few thyme leaves in each incision and turn the pork the right way up.

· Scatter the sliced onion in a shallow roasting tray and place the pork loin on top. Rub the skin with the honey and cinnamon glaze and season with the sea salt and some black pepper. Place in the oven for 15 minutes, then turn the heat down to 180°C/Fan 160°C/Gas 4 and pour the chicken stock into the base of the tray.

· Continue to roast for 1 hour 45 minutes, basting the pork with its juices every so often. Check to make sure it is properly cooked; the juices should run clear with no trace of pink when the flesh is pierced. Transfer the pork to a plate and cover with foil. Set aside for 20 minutes to rest.

· Spoon out the fat from the roasting tray and discard. Strain the meat juices into a small pan over a medium-low heat and whisk in the flour, making sure to get rid of any lumps. Simmer for a few minutes until the sauce thickens. Carve the pork into slices and serve with the gravy.

FISH
AND
SEAFOOD

Fish Soup with Chilli & Lime
GARUDHIYA, MALDIVES

Steamed Clams in Tomato Broth
BOUILLON TEC TEC, SEYCHELLES

Tilapia with Watercress & Tomato Sauce
TRONDRO GASY, MADAGASCAR

Stir-fried Crab, Pork & Lime
FOZA SY HENA-KISOA, MADAGASCAR

Maldivian Tuna Curry
DHON RIHA, MALDIVES

Ginger & Herb Grilled Red Snapper
SEYCHELLES

Mustard- & Turmeric-marinated Tuna
VINDAYE POISSON, MAURITIUS

Lobster in Vanilla Cream Sauce
LANGOUSTE À LA VANILLE, COMOROS & MAYOTTE

Creole Octopus Salad
SALADE OURITE, RODRIGUES

Sardines with Lemon, Chilli & Paprika
MAURITIUS

Fish Biryani
BRIYANI DE POISSON, MAURITIUS

Smoked Fish Salad with Peppers & Green Mango
SEYCHELLES

King Prawns with Tamarind & Coconut
CARI KOKO, SEYCHELLES

FISH
AND
SEAFOOD

WARM, PLANKTON-RICH, azure seas, coral reefs, mangrove forests and lagoons mean that fishing is at the very heart of life across the islands. More than two thousand species of fish swim in the Indian Ocean. Succulent octopus, sweet prawns (some tiny, some the size of your hand), lobster and crab are abundant. With a fresh catch taking little time to get from the teeming waters to the market stalls, everyday eating almost always involves some kind of marine life.

On these archipelagos and atolls, fish, crustaceans and molluscs are never far away, so they are rarely farmed. It means islanders feel a true connection to their seafood. Sometimes, when I'm on the beach, I chase the crabs as they poke up out of the sand, popping them into a bucket. My Uncle Sooresh taught me how to make a *bouillon* with them using tomatoes, vegetables and coriander leaves and some stock left over from cooking yesterday's fish – a reviving taste of the sea in a bowl.

With so much freshness available, it may surprise you to learn that islanders have an undying penchant for dried, salted and tinned fish. My mother always keeps a stack of Glenryck pilchards in their bright red tins in the cupboard, along with tins of tuna and sardines – that way she can whip up something really nutritious and tasty within minutes. She'll mash the contents with green chilli, lemon juice and finely chopped red onion and spread her creation onto some hot toast, or stuff tinned sardines into split peppers and bake for a tasty snack (p.163) – and I do the same. I also enjoy making moreish Sardine croquettes (p.178), where sardines are mashed with potatoes, thyme and chilli before being rolled into bite-size balls and fried until golden and crisp.

In this chapter I have created recipes for grills, coconut-infused curries, *briyani* (biryani) and *vindaye*, with mustard seeds, turmeric and wine vinegar. They're perfect for a light summer meal served alongside a bright, crisp salad, sliced baguette or just-made *roti* (p.138) to soak up those juices. Steam some rice and you have a plate of brightness to make you think of warmer climes. The dishes here use a particular type of fish or shellfish, but sometimes you can swap what I have stipulated for what your fishmonger has available and what is freshest. If you can't get a hold of the one I've suggested, then opt for something of equivalent texture: don't use an oily fish when the recipe calls for soft, white flesh – think halibut for tuna, snapper or sea bass for tilapia.

*Eaten almost every day in Maldivian home kitchens, this clear broth is simple
to make, and at once reviving, clean and refreshing.*

*The soup is sometimes eaten with taro (a root vegetable) or boiled breadfruit.
Alternatively it can be poured over a little rice and enjoyed with a squeeze of
lime, sliced raw onions and fresh chillies on the side, or simply brought to the
table as it is in the bowl. The crispy fried onions are my addition and add
a wonderfully crunchy texture that finishes off the dish.*

FISH SOUP WITH CHILLI & LIME
GARUDHIYA, MALDIVES

2 tsp sea salt
400g tuna steaks, cut into 2cm pieces
2–3 dried red chillies or 1 tsp
 chilli flakes
5 curry leaves
3 generous tbsp vegetable oil

1 onion, finely sliced
Juice of ½ lime

To serve:
Red chillies
1 lime, cut into wedges

SERVES:
4 AS A
STARTER,
2 AS A MAIN
PREP:
10 MINS
COOKING:
15 MINS

· Pour 1 litre cold water into a large saucepan and bring to the boil.
  Add the salt. Once it's at a rolling boil, add in the tuna pieces, chilli and
  curry leaves and let it boil for 5 minutes. Remove any greyish scum that
  rises to the top with a spoon.

· In the meantime, in a shallow frying pan, add the vegetable oil so it covers
  the bottom of the pan. Place over a medium-high heat. Add in the sliced
  onion and fry until it is golden brown and slightly charred. Take out and
  place onto a plate lined with kitchen paper to remove excess oil.

· Once the tuna is cooked throughout, check the broth for seasoning, adding
  more salt if needed. Squeeze over the lime juice and stir gently.

· Divide the soup into serving bowls, top with some crispy onions, extra red
  chillies if you wish and lime wedges. Serve immediately with rice or as it is.

In the Seychelles, tiny white shellfish called 'tec tec', or 'pipis', lie hidden in holes in the sand on the beach. Davide, a local Seychellois I met in Mahé, showed me how you can tap the holes gently with your feet and, like magic, the 'tec tec' will appear. A delicacy on the island, these freshly caught shellfish are cooked in a garlicky tomato broth, calling for a hunk of bread to soak up the sea juices.

I have suggested mussels as a suitable alternative for this soup. Check the shells are undamaged and tightly shut (or close when tapped) just before cooking commences to make sure they are fresh. A quick rinse under cold running water to remove any grit is a good idea.

STEAMED CLAMS IN TOMATO BROTH
BOULLON TEC TEC, SEYCHELLES

500g clams or mussels,
    beards removed, scrubbed and
    cleaned (discard any open shells)
3 tbsp vegetable oil
2 shallots, finely chopped
3 garlic cloves, finely chopped
2.5cm piece of fresh root ginger,
    peeled and grated
2 thyme sprigs, leaves picked
2 ripe tomatoes (200g),
    roughly chopped

50ml good-quality white wine
400ml reserved clam/mussel
    cooking liquid topped up
    with water
1 tbsp finely chopped parsley
Sea salt and freshly ground
    black pepper

To serve:
1 lemon, cut into wedges
Crusty bread or baguette

SERVES:
2
PREP:
25 MINS
COOK:
15 MINS

- Place a large saucepan with 100ml water over a medium-high heat. Once it comes to the boil, tip in the clams and place the lid on top. Steam the clams for 2 minutes until the shells have opened. Give the pan a little shake to encourage any remaining closed ones to open. Take off the heat, strain the clam liquid into a jug and top up with water to 400ml. Discard any clams that don't open.

- Place another large saucepan over a medium heat, pour in the oil and tip in the shallots, garlic, ginger and thyme. Sauté for 3–5 minutes until softened, stirring occasionally.

- Stir the chopped tomatoes, wine and reserved clam stock into the pan. Let this gently simmer for 5 minutes for the flavours to mix together.

- The liquid should now have reduced slightly. Add the clams back into the pan and simmer for another 2 minutes. Check for seasoning, scatter over the parsley leaves and serve in bowls with lemon wedges and crusty bread.

Tilapia, a freshwater fish delicate in taste and meaty in texture, is a favourite of Malagasy cuisine. This recipe originates from the Sakalava region on the west coast of Madagascar and the name refers to the 'people of the long valleys and rivers' living in the vast plains and rolling foothills.

Make sure your tomatoes are ripe and juicy to make this dish really sing. Serve over steamed rice.

TILAPIA WITH WATERCRESS & TOMATO SAUCE
TRONDRO GASY, MADAGASCAR

1kg tilapia, cod or pollock
  (cut into steaks 2.5cm wide:
  ask your fishmonger to do this)
1 lemon, juice of ½ and the rest cut
  into wedges
2 tbsp olive oil
1 large onion, finely sliced
4 ripe tomatoes (approx. 375g),
  roughly chopped
2 garlic cloves, finely chopped

1 tbsp medium curry powder
85g watercress, chopped
Sea salt and freshly ground
  black pepper

To serve:
1 bunch of spring onions,
  finely chopped
2 tbsp finely chopped coriander

SERVES:
4
PREP:
20 MINS
COOK:
25 MINS

· First wash the fish, pat dry with kitchen paper and place in a bowl. Squeeze over the lemon juice and season with salt and pepper. Set aside.

· In a large frying or sauté pan over a medium heat, drizzle in the olive oil, add in the sliced onion and sweat for 5–7 minutes until translucent and softened. Next add in the chopped tomatoes, ½ teaspoon pepper, 1 teaspoon salt and the garlic and let this cook, stirring occasionally, for a further 5 minutes. The tomatoes will break down and release their pinkish juices into the sauce. At this point add in the curry powder. Give it a good stir.

· Add in 100ml water and let this cook for another 2 minutes before creating a space in the centre of the pan, using your spoon to push the sauce to the sides, and place all the chopped watercress in the middle.

· Next put all the tilapia steaks around the watercress, gently nestling them into the tomato sauce. Turn down the heat to a medium-low simmer, cover the pan with a lid and let this cook gently for 8 minutes, turning over the tilapia steaks halfway through to get coated in the sauce. When the fish is white, opaque and flaking when forked, it is ready to serve.

· Scatter over finely chopped spring onion and coriander and serve alongside the lemon wedges with some steamed basmati rice.

A heaped plateful of this invigorating spiced ginger and lime stir-fried crab, mingled with pork and fresh greens, is irresistible. The sour citrus, fiery chilli and fermented saltiness of the fish sauce complement each other beautifully.

You can buy ready-prepared white crab meat in the supermarkets and online. If you are using fresh, check the note below. Serve with white rice and a generous squeeze of lime juice for an uplifting zing.

STIR-FRIED CRAB, PORK & LIME
FOZA SY HENA-KISOA, MADAGASCAR

2 tbsp vegetable oil
1 large onion, finely sliced
3 garlic cloves, finely chopped
2.5cm piece of fresh root ginger, peeled and finely chopped
250g minced pork
2 green chillies, finely chopped
2 tbsp dark soy sauce
1 tbsp fish sauce

250g white crab meat
(1–1.5kg whole cooked crab yields approx. 250g fresh meat)
(*see note opposite*)
80g spring greens, kale or spinach, roughly chopped
Juice of 1 lime
2 spring onions, finely chopped
1 lime, cut into wedges, to serve

SERVES:
4
PREP:
20 MINS
(PLUS 40 MINS
IF PREPARING
YOUR OWN
CRAB)
COOK:
10 MINS

- Place a large wok over a medium-high heat and add the vegetable oil. Tip in the onion, garlic and ginger and cook for around 3–5 minutes until softened but not browning. Stir continuously to keep them moving around the pan.

- Add in the pork and chillies, breaking up the meat as you stir with your spoon, and fry for 5 minutes until it's a light brown colour. Pour in the soy sauce and fish sauce. At this point scatter over the crab meat and spring greens. Mix well and cook for 2 minutes more, stirring frequently, until the greens have wilted. Squeeze over the lime juice and scatter over the spring onions to finish. Serve with the lime wedges, and some white rice.

How to prepare a whole crab

- Crabs are best cooked immediately: you can purchase them fresh from your fishmonger (never buy a dead uncooked crab as you do not know how long it will be safe to eat). Put the crab in the freezer for about 20 minutes before you're ready to cook.

- Bring a large pan of salted water to the boil. Take your crab from the freezer, lift the triangular flap in the centre of its undercarriage and, using a skewer, pierce through the small indentation there. Pierce again through the crab's mouth, between and below the eyes. Drop the crab into the boiling water and simmer for 12 minutes per kg. Leave to cool a little, then transfer to a tray placed in the fridge to cool completely.

- Use your palm to push down on the crab, pull apart the shell and discard the feathery gills (dead man's fingers). With a spoon, scoop out the brown meat. Crack open the claws and legs, then pick out the white meat from the cavities (keep an eye out for any bits of shell). It's now ready to use.

RODRIGUES

REMOTE, RUSTIC AND wild, the tiny, volcanic outcrop of Rodrigues feels like a place where time has stood still. A dependency of Mauritius, lying 622km east, it is a lovely contrast to its bigger, brasher neighbour – drier, rockier and with no sugar cane plantations at all, its tranquility, mesmerising natural beauty and smiling people make it a little off-the-beaten-track paradise.

Small it may be – just eleven miles by five and with a population of 40,000 people – but Rodrigues stands up to the rest of the Indian Ocean islands in terms of cuisine. The staple food is fish from the surrounding aquamarine lagoon – there's bekin, wahoo, mullet, crab and prawns. The most totemic seafood here is octopus (*poulpe*). You'll see local straw-hatted women known as *piqueuses d'ourite* wading, holding a long spike and searching for the tentacled beasts that swim in these waters. They follow the rhythm of the tides, and when they are done they gut their catch and hang them across wooden poles to dry in the sun for five days before selling them at the market – the salty meat is used to bring a pungency to *mazavaroo*, a dried red chilli paste. Fresh, undried octopus is cooked in a curry known as *vindaye* with mustard and turmeric or in a Creole salad.

Rodrigues relies on subsistence living: every family tends to have a little vegetable plot, some fruit trees and free-range chickens, pigs and goats. Many homes keep their own bees and make honey which is super sweet and incredibly pure because there is very little pollution. The island has its own special little lemon, known as *limon bittersweet* or *citron galet*, meaning 'lemon pebble'; it can be confited, used to make lemonade and features in many of the local desserts.

You can tell much about a place, particularly an island, by a visit to a Saturday market. It's worth getting up early for the one at the little capital town Port Mathurin to experience a more bustling side to the usually sleepy routine. There's an energetic buzz because this is a social time, where people gather to sell their wares or buy fresh produce and share stories, jokes and a snack. Red beans (*haricots rouges*) spill out of bags, there's corn-fed chicken, local hams, jars of honey and *ti pots* – small pots of *limon* and pickled fruits and vegetables in a spicy chilli sauce flavoured with ginger or crystallised lemon – as well as bottles crammed with hundreds of hot *piments* (tiny chillies) preserved in oil. By noon the market starts to wind down, the streets empty and the island slowly drips into its daily afternoon slumber.

The best way to eat out in Rodrigues is to find a *table d'hôte* (host's table) meal where you will be welcomed into a local home for a buffet of the best food the island has to offer. My absolute favourite is the speciality dessert of the island *la tourte rodriguaise*, a thick-crust pie with a jammy filling of coconut and papaya.

Port Mathurin

RODRIGUES

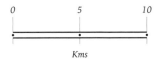

0   5   10

Kms

This warm, tangy fish curry is cooled with mellow coconut milk. It celebrates two cherished ingredients in Maldivian cuisine: tuna and coconut. The latter is served at almost every meal, whether the milk is extracted and added to curries like this or it is freshly grated or sliced and used as a condiment.

The tuna is enhanced with southern Indian spices including cardamom, curry leaves and turmeric. It doesn't take long to cook, so this dish can be ready to eat in under thirty minutes, perfect for a midweek meal with steamed rice. 'Dhon riha' is also enjoyed at breakfast by locals, served with rice, chillies and 'roshi' (thin Maldivian flatbreads) or my Island-style rotis (p.138) on the side, which are perfect for scooping up the sauce.

MALDIVIAN TUNA CURRY
DHON RIHA, MALDIVES

500g tuna steak, cut into 2.5cm pieces
1 tbsp coconut oil
4 garlic cloves, finely chopped
2 cardamom pods, seeds only, crushed
2.5cm piece of fresh root ginger, peeled and finely chopped
10 curry leaves, finely chopped
1 green chilli, finely sliced
1 onion, finely sliced

½ tsp ground fennel seeds
½ tsp ground cumin
½ tsp ground turmeric
½ tsp black pepper
400ml tin coconut milk
1 cinnamon stick
Sea salt
Coriander, to garnish

SERVES:
2–4
PREP:
15 MINS
COOK:
15 MINS

- Lightly salt the fish and set aside.

- In a large saucepan, warm the coconut oil over a medium heat until simmering. Add in the garlic, cardamom, ginger, curry leaves and chilli. Let this sauté until fragrant – usually around 30 seconds. Add the onion slices and cook until softened, around 5–7 minutes. Add the rest of the spices: the fennel, cumin, turmeric and black pepper. After around a minute they will mingle together and become aromatic.

- At this point, transfer everything into a food processor and blend to a coarse paste. Return the paste back to the pan over a medium heat, pour in the coconut milk, holding back one tablespoon for drizzling at the end, and pop in the cinnamon stick and ½ teaspoon salt.

- Bring to a simmer and gently add the fish pieces to the sauce. They will cook fairly quickly. After 5 minutes, the fish should be tender, opaque and cooked throughout and the curry will be ready to serve. Drizzle over the extra coconut milk, scatter with the coriander and serve with a heap of rice.

Witnessing the majestic 'bourzwa' (red snapper) being brought to shore by local fishermen on Grand Anse beach in Mahé is an awe-inspiring sight. The fish's iridescent skin glints in the sun, pale pink and orange; it is a prize catch.

Here the fish is grilled until crispy and charred, and I like to add lemons, parsley and chillies to give a flash of warm spice and a cooling, herby aftertaste. Serve with papaya chutney, boiled breadfruit or Creole saffran rice (p.131).

GINGER & HERB GRILLED RED SNAPPER
SEYCHELLES

2 x 600g red snapper or red bream, gutted and cleaned
1 tsp ground turmeric
Sea salt and freshly ground black pepper

For the marinade:
3 green chillies, roughly chopped
5cm piece of fresh root ginger, peeled and roughly chopped
3 garlic cloves, roughly chopped
4 thyme sprigs, leaves picked
Large handful of parsley, leaves and stalks chopped

Juice of 2 lemons
½ tsp sea salt
2 tbsp olive oil, plus extra for drizzling

For the inside of the fish:
1 lemon, sliced
1 small bunch of parsley

To serve:
1 lemon, cut into wedges
1 lime, cut into wedges

SERVES:
4
PREP:
10 MINS, PLUS 30 MINS MARINATING
COOK:
20 MINS

- Take your snappers and place on a large baking tray. Make three to four slashes with a knife, 1cm deep into the fish, and repeat on the other side on both of them. Season the fish well with salt, pepper and turmeric on both sides, rubbing it into the skin, the slashes and inside the fish.

- In a blender whiz all the marinade ingredients together until a coarse, green, spicy paste is achieved. Pour this over the fish and rub in well too, including inside the fish. Stuff the cavity with lemon slices and parsley. Cover with cling film and marinate in the fridge for 30 minutes.

- Preheat your oven to grill function or heat a barbecue. Drizzle the fish with olive oil and oil the grill tray using some kitchen roll to stop the fish from sticking. You can also cook it on a baking tray lined with foil.

- Place the fish under the hot grill (or sear on the barbecue) for 3–5 minutes on each side until charred. Finish off in a preheated oven at 180°C/Fan 160°C/Gas 4 for 10 minutes or so until cooked throughout and the flesh is white and opaque. Finally season with salt and pepper. Serve immediately with lemon and lime wedges to squeeze over.

*A recipe with a winding, colonial history and a unique cooking method –
the fish pieces are gently cooked in oil, then marinated in all the spices and
vinegar and left in the fridge to soak up the robust flavours. The resulting fish
is a luminous yellow, heady and fragrant with turmeric, mustard seeds, green
chillies, garlic and onions. Its flavours ignite the palate.*

*I make this pickled mustard fish the day before I want to eat it as the spices
permeate the fish overnight, then let it come to room temperature before eating.*

*You can use fresh tuna, any firm white fish or pieces of octopus and prawns
with this spice mix. I eat it stuffed into a fresh crusty baguette, or with rice.*

MUSTARD- & TURMERIC-MARINATED TUNA
VINDAYE POISSON, MAURITIUS

700g tuna, trevally or king fish steaks
  (ask your fishmonger to clean and
  cut to approx. 2.5cm thickness)
2 tbsp ground turmeric
2 tbsp black mustard seeds
4 tbsp mustard oil (or vegetable oil)
4 garlic cloves, finely chopped

2 onions, thinly sliced
6–8 green chillies, split lengthways,
  deseeded
100ml vegetable oil
3 tbsp white wine vinegar
Sea salt and freshly ground
  black pepper

SERVES:
4
PREP:
25 MINS,
PLUS
OVERNIGHT
MARINATING
COOK:
15 MINS

· Season the fish with salt and pepper.

· Using a pestle and mortar, grind the turmeric and black mustard seeds
  together. Add a splash of water to make a coarse paste.

· Place a frying pan on a medium-high heat and pour in 2 tablespoons of the
  mustard oil.

· Fry the fish for 4–5 minutes on each side or until just cooked through and
  slightly crisp. Drain on kitchen paper, leave to cool slightly, then cut into
  bite-size pieces and place in a mixing bowl.

· At this point I don't wipe the pan down but instead keep the tuna's flavour
  in there for making the paste. Add the remaining 2 tablespoons of mustard
  oil to the pan, tip in the garlic, onion and chillies and cook for 1 minute.
  Spoon in the spice paste and fry for 30 seconds, stirring well into the oil.
  Add the fish pieces and gently incorporate with the yellow-tinged spice
  mix until every piece is coated. Take off the heat and pour in the vegetable
  oil, 1 teaspoon salt and the vinegar, and mix again.

· Allow to cool, cover in an airtight container and leave to marinate in the
  fridge overnight where it will keep for 2–3 days. Take it out of the fridge
  10 minutes before serving to come up to room temperature and give it a
  gentle stir again before eating.

This is the luxurious national dish of Comoros: rich, tender lobster paired with a smooth sauce made from white wine, shallots and butter (you can detect the French influence here). The lobster is either grilled on an open flame or simmered in the sauce. The special ingredient is the locally harvested vanilla pod, which adds a delicate dose of natural sweetness.

If you're feeling adventurous you can prepare your own shellfish stock and live lobster for this dish (see notes opposite). Alternatively, fresh fish stock is available in supermarkets and you can get your fishmonger to prepare the lobster for you. You can also use langoustines as an alternative to lobster. This is an indulgent recipe and certainly a dish for a special occasion.

LOBSTER IN VANILLA CREAM SAUCE
LANGOUSTE À LA VANILLE, COMOROS & MAYOTTE

2 tbsp unsalted butter
2 shallots, finely diced
1 vanilla pod, split lengthways
100ml good-quality dry white wine
250ml shellfish stock (*see note opposite*), or use shop-bought fish stock
75ml double cream

100g spinach
2 lobsters (approx. 700g each) (*see note opposite*), cut in half lengthways
Olive oil, for drizzling
Sea salt and freshly ground black pepper

SERVES:
4
PREP:
25 MINS
(PLUS 45 MINS
IF MAKING
YOUR OWN
STOCK)
COOK:
25 MINS

• First make the sauce by melting the butter in a medium saucepan over a medium heat. Add in the shallots and sauté for 5 minutes until softened, then add in the vanilla pod.

• Pour in the white wine, leave to bubble away until it is reduced by half, then add the stock. Simmer until the sauce has reduced by half and intensified in flavour. Remove the vanilla pod.

• Pour the sauce into a blender and whiz until smooth, then tip it back into the pan on a low heat. Slowly whisk in the double cream until it starts to thicken. Drop in the spinach and let it wilt for a couple of minutes. Check the sauce for seasoning and set aside.

- Season the lobster halves with salt and pepper and preheat a grill pan over a medium-high heat. Drizzle olive oil over the lobster halves and place flesh side down on the pan until slightly charred, then flip over onto the other side to do the same. Grill for around 5 minutes per side. To see if the lobster is cooked, try removing the flesh. If it comes out without any resistance, it is cooked.

- Place on serving plates and spoon over some of the spinach and sauce. Serve immediately with rice.

How to prepare a lobster

- You should kill your lobster just before cooking it. The most humane way to do this is to put it in the freezer for 1 hour. Then, having made sure that the lobster is no longer moving, push the tip of a large, sharp, heavy knife through the centre of the cross on its head to kill it instantly.

- Alternatively, you can source pre-cooked lobsters online (see p.256). Slice them in half lengthways and they are ready to use. They will simply need to be warmed through on the grill before the sauce is added.

How to make shellfish stock

- The shellfish stock can be prepared fresh by roasting any bones or heads of shellfish in the oven (such as lobster shells or prawns) at 180°C/Fan 160°C/Gas 4 for 15 minutes, turning them over halfway. Place in a large saucepan with some carrot, celery, leek, onion, thyme and bay leaves covered with water, bring to the boil and simmer for 30 minutes. Pass through a sieve and you will have a flavourful stock. Store in the fridge for a couple of days or pour into an ice cube tray and freeze for easy access for cooking. It will last for up to a month.

Pictured overleaf

Rodrigues lies in a shallow lagoon and octopuses love to hide in the tiny nooks and cracks in the rocks. Fisherwomen, known as 'piqueuses d'ourite', wade through low tide, hunting for octopus with metal spears. Once caught the octopus is sold fresh in the market or sun-dried – stretched onto sticks until it's ready to be sold.

You can buy octopus at a fishmonger, fresh or frozen, or order it online. To tenderise the octopus, freeze it beforehand and defrost overnight, which helps break down the tissues. When prepared and cooked the right way, the meat can be juicy and tender, similar to lobster. This dish lets the freshness of the octopus speak for itself, complemented by a vibrant, colourful salad.

CREOLE OCTOPUS SALAD
SALADE OURITE, RODRIGUES

1 tbsp salt
1kg octopus, head and beak removed
   (when cooking be prepared for
   about 30% shrinkage)
1 bay leaf
1 tbsp black peppercorns
1 red pepper, diced
1 green chilli, finely sliced
1 ripe tomato, seeds discarded, diced
1 spring onion, finely chopped
2 tbsp chopped flat-leaf parsley

1 small mango, peeled and diced
  (see note on p.14)
Sea salt and freshly ground
  black pepper
Salad of spinach leaves, to serve

For the dressing:
Juice of 1 lemon
2 tbsp olive oil
1 tsp honey
½ tsp sea salt
½ tsp freshly ground black pepper

SERVES:
2 (OR 4
AS A SMALL
STARTER)
PREP:
15 MINS
PLUS AT LEAST
15 MINS
MARINATING
COOK:
1 HOUR

- Fill a large cooking pot with water, add the 1 tablespoon salt and bring to the boil. Add the octopus, bay leaf and peppercorns, lower the heat to a gentle simmer, cover and cook gently for 45–60 minutes until tender.

- Meanwhile, in a large mixing bowl, add the pepper, chilli, tomato, spring onion, parsley and mango. Give this all a gentle stir.

- Next make the dressing: in a small bowl, squeeze in the lemon juice, olive oil and honey and season with the salt and pepper. Give this a good mix.

- Take out the octopus when tender, place on a chopping board and sprinkle with sea salt. Leave to cool slightly. Cut the meat into diagonal 1cm pieces and add to the mixing bowl with the vegetables.

- Pour over the dressing and gently mix together. Leave the salad in the fridge for the flavours to mingle for 1 hour (or at least 15 minutes).

- Serve on a bed of spinach leaves with a glass of crisp white wine.

My Uncle Sooresh sets off at dawn to get the best pick of fish for the day, most of which is cooked at his café-style restaurant on the east coast of Mauritius. As children we were the fortunate recipients of the surplus, ready to be cooked on the barbecue that evening on the beach or in my aunt's kitchen.

This recipe is inspired by those suppers. I love flaking the charred fish between my fingers, squeezing over lashings of lemon and using my hands to scoop it up with some rice. This recipe relies upon very fresh fish, so it's best to source the sardines from your fishmonger.

SARDINES WITH LEMON, CHILLI & PAPRIKA
MAURITIUS

3 tbsp olive oil
1 tbsp paprika
Zest and juice of 1 lemon
2.5cm piece of fresh root ginger, peeled and grated
4 garlic cloves, finely chopped

2 green chillies, finely chopped
½ tsp freshly ground black pepper
8 fresh sardines, cleaned and scaled
2 tbsp chopped coriander
Sea salt
Lemon wedges, to serve

SERVES:
4
PREP:
15 MINS
COOK:
10 MINS

• Mix together the oil, paprika, lemon, ginger, garlic, chillies and black pepper in a bowl. Using a sharp knife, make shallow slashes in the fish on both sides and rub the marinade all over and into the grooves.

• Preheat the grill to a medium-high heat.

• Place the fish on a baking tray lined with lightly oiled foil and place under the grill for 3–5 minutes on one side, then turn over onto the other for another 3–5 minutes (keep a close eye on the fish as timings on oven grills will vary). Ensure the skin is slightly charred on both sides and the fish is cooked throughout. Lay on a plate and serve scattered with coriander, a sprinkle of sea salt and a few lemon wedges.

• Eat with crusty bread or rice.

When in Mauritius, a 'briyani' is a must-try. It is sold everywhere, in restaurants and by sellers in the market from conical deg pots, which are heated over a slow fire. This fragrant rice dish dates back to the Mogul Empire and has Hyderabadi and Pakistani roots from the days of Bandari seafarers settling in Port Louis, seeding their style of cuisine into Mauritian culture.

'Briyanis' are known for taking a long time to prepare, but here I have used fish instead of meat as it cooks more quickly and still makes for an exciting dish. The marinade of turmeric, chillies, coriander and yoghurt adds an aromatic depth of flavour, while the saffron lends an earthy yet floral spicing, and the charred sticky onions draw together all the layers. Serve alongside a Ripe tomato salad with chilli & lemon (p.109) or a Green bean, cabbage & carrot mustard pickle (p.186).

FISH BIRYANI
BRIYANI DE POISSON, MAURITIUS

500g basmati rice
Large pinch of saffron strands
500g skinless cod fillet
(or any firm white fish fillets),
cut into 2.5cm chunks
1 cinnamon stick
2 tsp sea salt
1 bay leaf
Vegetable oil, for frying
2 tbsp ghee
2 onions, sliced
2 medium potatoes (approx. 400g),
peeled and cut into 2.5cm cubes
1 small bunch of coriander,
leaves picked and chopped
1 small bunch of mint,
leaves picked and chopped
60g fresh or frozen peas

For the marinade:
200ml natural yoghurt
2.5cm piece of fresh root ginger,
peeled and finely chopped
2 garlic cloves, finely chopped
3 red chillies, deseeded and
finely chopped
1 tsp ground turmeric
2 tsp sea salt
1 small bunch of coriander,
leaves and stalks finely chopped

For the spice mix:
1 tsp ground cinnamon
4 curry leaves, finely chopped
4 cloves
3 cardamom pods, seeds only, crushed
½ tsp ground nutmeg
1 heaped tsp cumin seeds
1 tsp coriander seeds

SERVES:
4–6
PREP:
1 HOUR
15 MINS
COOK:
45 MINS,
PLUS
10 MINS
RESTING

- Soak the rice for 30 minutes in cold water (or wash a few times until the water runs clear). Soak the saffron in 200ml hot water and set aside.

- Place the fish chunks in a large mixing bowl, add in all the marinade ingredients and mix well together. Set aside while you make the spice mix.

- Add all the spice mix ingredients to a small frying pan over a medium-high heat for 30 seconds–1 minute, until toasted and aromatic, taking care not to burn them.

- Place the toasted spices in a spice grinder or use a pestle and mortar to pound to a fine powder. Tip into the bowl with the fish and marinade, and combine well. Cover the bowl with cling film and leave in the fridge for 30 minutes for the flavours to infuse the fish.

- Next take the soaked rice, drain it and rinse it a couple of times until the water runs clear. Add to a saucepan with about 2 litres water, the cinnamon stick, salt and bay leaf. Bring to the boil and simmer, covered, for 5 minutes until half cooked. Drain, removing the bay leaf and the cinnamon stick, and rinse again with cold water to stop the cooking process. Set aside.

- Now prepare the fried onions: add about 5–6 tablespoons vegetable oil plus 1 tablespoon ghee to a large frying pan. Place on a medium-high heat, wait for the ghee to melt, and drop in the sliced onion (you might have to do this in batches). Fry until the onion is brown and crisp all over, around 7–10 minutes (a little burnt is ok as it adds to the flavour of the *briyani*). Drain using a slotted spoon and place on a plate lined with kitchen paper. Repeat with the remaining onion and set aside.

- In the same pan on a medium-high heat, fry the potatoes. Drop in the potato cubes and cook until golden brown all over and nearly tender, around 15 minutes. Drain on a plate lined with kitchen paper.

- To assemble, grease the bottom of a large, deep saucepan (with a lid) with a little bit of oil. Add in a layer (about a third) of the rice, covering the bottom of the pan. Pour the fish and its marinade over the rice. Next scatter over half the fried onions, all of the potatoes and half the coriander and mint leaves. Layer over the rest of the rice. Sprinkle over the rest of the onions, the green peas (it's fine if using frozen, they will steam while cooking) and remaining mint and coriander leaves. Pour over the saffron and soaking water. Dot the remaining 1 tablespoon of ghee over the top of the rice. Cover tightly with foil and place the lid on top.

- Put the dish over a medium heat for 15 minutes, then take off the heat and let it sit for 10 minutes. Open up and fork the rice; the water should have evaporated and the potatoes and fish should be cooked throughout. Serve immediately.

Pictured overleaf

A delicacy in the Seychelles, this dish is simple and endlessly adaptable. The star of the show is the smoked fish. Typically swordfish, sailfish or marlin are used, but I love it with smoked mackerel. Green mangoes can be found in most Asian grocers and add a sour, crunchy tang and a pleasant contrast to the sweet peppers. If you can't source them, it's fine to use green papaya or a slightly under-ripe mango you might find in the supermarket.

This dish reminds me of summer picnics on the island, sitting with bare feet nestled in the warm sand, and a Tupperware full of this refreshing salad. All it calls for is some crusty buttered bread and something chilled to drink alongside.

SMOKED FISH SALAD WITH PEPPERS & GREEN MANGO
SEYCHELLES

1 x 240g pack smoked mackerel
1 red pepper, finely chopped
4 tomatoes (350g), finely chopped
1 small onion, thinly sliced
1 green mango, peeled and thinly sliced (*see note on p.14*)
3 tbsp extra virgin olive oil

Handful of coriander, leaves finely chopped
Handful of flat-leaf parsley, leaves finely chopped
Juice of 1 lemon
Sea salt and freshly ground black pepper

SERVES:
4 AS A LIGHT LUNCH
PREP:
15 MINS

- First peel the skin off the mackerel, scrape away any dark brown flesh, then flake into a large mixing bowl. Add in the pepper, tomato, onion and mango, drizzle with the olive oil, season with salt and black pepper, scatter over the chopped herbs and squeeze over the lemon juice. Give the ingredients a good mix until everything is combined and serve piled onto a plate with buttered crusty bread.

In the Seychelles they love their curries hot and spicy, with lashings of coconut milk – in fact it's unheard of not to add coconut to a curry (you will get surprised looks). Here I have freshly ground the spices to make a traditional Seychellois 'massalé' – and it packs a punch. It is also used in the Seychellois aubergine & chickpea cari (p.119). Tamarind pulp is made from the flesh inside the tamarind pod, and the brown-red concentrate has a sticky, date-like consistency that is tart and sour, heightening the flavour in salads, curries and even desserts. I love the fleshy prawns, sweet coconut and tangy tamarind combination here. Serve it with rice, a fresh salad and your favourite chilli sauce or chutney.

KING PRAWNS WITH TAMARIND & COCONUT
CARI KOKO, SEYCHELLES

15–20 fresh raw king prawns
   (350g), peeled, deveined
   and cleaned
3 tbsp vegetable oil
1 onion, sliced
3 garlic cloves, finely chopped
2.5cm piece of fresh root ginger,
   peeled and grated
2 green chillies, split lengthways
5 curry leaves
½ tsp ground turmeric
1 tsp tomato purée or 1 tomato, diced
3 tbsp tamarind paste or pulp
   (*see note opposite*)
400ml tin coconut milk
Sea salt and freshly ground
   black pepper

For the Seychellois 'massalé':
2 tbsp coriander seeds
2 tsp cumin seeds
2 tsp black peppercorns
6 cardamom pods, seeds only
½ tsp cloves
1 cinnamon stick or
   1 tsp ground cinnamon
1 tsp chilli powder
1 tsp grated nutmeg

To serve:
1 tbsp chopped flat-leaf parsley
1 lime, cut into wedges

SERVES:
2
PREP:
15 MINS
COOK:
25 MINS

· First make the *massalé*. In a small pan over a medium-high heat, dry-roast the coriander seeds, cumin seeds, black peppercorns, cardamom seeds, cloves and cinnamon for 30 seconds until aromatic, being careful not to let them burn. Grind all the dry ingredients in a spice grinder or pulverise using a pestle and mortar. Add in the chilli powder and nutmeg. Place in an airtight jar and keep for future use (this will make more than you need in this recipe).

· Season the prawns with salt and pepper, and set aside.

· Heat the oil in a deep saucepan on a medium-high heat. Fry the onion for 3–4 minutes until softened, then add in the garlic, ginger, chillies and

curry leaves to cook for a few minutes until fragrant. Mix in 2 tablespoons of the *massalé*, the turmeric and the tomato, stirring gently. Pour in the tamarind and coconut milk and simmer for 15 minutes until the sauce has thickened and reduced. Add in the prawns and ½ teaspoon salt and cook for 5 minutes until they are opaque and tender.

· Check the seasoning and, to finish, garnish with parsley and lime wedges.

Note

· You can find concentrated tamarind blocks or fresh pods in most Asian stores. In the supermarket you will also find tamarind paste (a bit more watery), which is fine to use as it is. For guidance on preparing tamarind blocks or fresh pods, see p.20.

VEGETABLES
AND
SIDES

Tamarind Pineapple Chilli Salt Salad
MAURITIUS

Okra & Tomato Salad with Red Onion
LALO SALADE, MAURITIUS

Ripe Tomato Salad with Chilli & Lemon
SATINI POMME D'AMOUR, MAURITIUS

Toasted Coconut, Mango & Carrot Salad
MAURITIUS

Watercress & Pak Choi Broth
BOUILLON CRESSON, MAURITIUS

Creamy Sweet Potato Soup
COMOROS & MAYOTTE

Seychellois Aubergine & Chickpea Cari
SEYCHELLES

Pumpkin & Chou Chou Gratin
GRATIN DE CHOU CHOU, RÉUNION

Braised Aubergine with Potatoes & Chilli
TOUFFÉ BRINGEL, MAURITIUS

Creamy Lentils with Thyme & Turmeric
RÉUNION

Kidney Bean, Butternut & Potato Stew
LA DAUBE, MAURITIUS

Mum's Spicy Mashed Potato
SATINI POMME DE TERRE, MAURITIUS

Malagasy Coconut Rice
VARY AMIN'NY VOANIO, MADAGASCAR

Creole Saffran Rice
SEYCHELLES

Mauritian Fried Rice with Vegetables
RIZ FRIT, MAURITIUS

Curry Leaf Bread Rolls
SEYCHELLES

Island-style Rotis
ALL ISLANDS

VEGETABLES
AND
SIDES

THANKS TO THE glorious sunshine and rich, fertile soil of the Indian Ocean islands, they are abundant with vegetables, pulses and grains. Fresh produce ranges from the exotic to the more everyday – all grown in local farms, back yards or imported from other islands across the seas. Visiting the vibrant local markets is a spectacle in itself, a veritable feast for the senses as you take in the array of coloured vegetables, baskets of Day-Glo chillies, bunches of fresh herbs and intricately carved pineapples, the tables crammed with produce fresh from the fields of the island, still glistening with dew. The air is filled with the sound of bartering and the heady aroma of spices as locals mingle amongst tourists, picking the best produce for the day; you won't find fresher anywhere else.

There are always vegetables in some shape or form on the dinner table, whether it's a light and refreshing salad to accompany grilled and barbecued meats or a wholesome vegetable side dish, such as the Pumpkin & chou chou gratin from Réunion (p.120). But many of the dishes can be fulfilling meals in themselves; the famous Mauritian dish *touffé*, Braised aubergine with potatoes & chilli (p.123), is a beautifully simple dish when served with a bowl of plain rice, as is the French-inspired *daube* or kidney bean stew (p.126). In fact,

a meal isn't quite complete without a bowl of steaming, fluffy fragrant rice, and *vary* (the Malagasy word for rice) is often eaten a few times a day! This can be simply plain, dotted with aromatics like cinnamon and cardamom, or brightened with yellow turmeric (Creole saffran rice, p.131), fried with diced vegetables or made creamy and sweet with coconut milk (p.128). However, rice isn't the only staple carbohydrate. Bread, in its many forms, from fresh *rotis* (p.138), *chapatis*, *puris*, *roshi* (Maldivian bread) and baguettes, are all eaten alongside the dishes of these islands, either to scoop up handfuls of *cari* or to soak up leftover sauce, often replacing the need for cutlery. These are best eaten as soon as they are made.

What I love about these recipes is their versatility; you can choose any one of them to complement so many of the other dishes in this book. So enjoy the fruits of the land, bursting with sunshine, goodness and flavour from the tropics.

This is my take on a popular street food in Mauritius: small, juicy 'Victoria' (named after the British queen) pineapples are peeled, placed in cellophane bags and shaken with red chilli, sea salt and tamarind pulp. It's the most refreshing snack to enjoy whilst walking barefoot down the beach. When I've made this for friends their eyes light up with the surprise of the scorching chilli, the sourness of the tamarind and the sweet juices of the pineapple. This is a fabulous salad that goes well with anything grilled or barbecued and can also be eaten as an alternative dessert.

TAMARIND PINEAPPLE CHILLI SALT SALAD
MAURITIUS

1 pineapple (800g), peeled and diced (*see note on p.14*)
½ cucumber (150g), diced
1 mango, peeled and cut into dice (*see note on p.14*)
1 tsp soft light brown sugar

1 tsp tamarind pulp or paste (*see note below*)
½ tsp sea salt
1 tsp chilli flakes or 1 red chilli, sliced

SERVES:
6
PREP:
15 MINS, PLUS 1 HOUR MARINATING

• Place the pineapple, cucumber and mango in a large mixing bowl and mix well with a large spoon. Scatter in the brown sugar and tamarind paste and combine.

• Using a pestle and mortar, pound your salt and chilli until it's a red- and white-flecked grainy salt.

• Add the chilli salt to the mixing bowl and combine well. Cover and let it sit in the fridge for 1 hour to marinate before eating.

Note

• You can find concentrated tamarind blocks or fresh pods in most Asian stores. In the supermarket you will also find tamarind paste (a bit more watery), which is fine to use as it is. For guidance on preparing tamarind blocks or fresh pods, see p.20.

Okra, also known by the faintly alarming name 'ladies' fingers' (referring to their long elegant shape), have a mild flavour similar to aubergine. They can be cooked whole or chopped and simply sautéed, used to thicken stews (because of the sticky liquid they produce when cooked), pickled or fried until crispy.

My mum would buy these daily from the local Asian shop and sauté them with garlic, ginger, thyme and a little tomato. I like them with a little more bite, and this salad is perfect as a side dish to some fish, grilled meat or even a 'cari'. The crunch of the okra with a tangy vinegar dressing and heat from the chilli work in exceptional harmony, but it's those crispy fried breadcrumbs speckled on top that complete this fabulously textured salad. You can buy okra at large supermarkets, or in Asian stores.

OKRA & TOMATO SALAD WITH RED ONION
LALO SALADE, MAURITIUS

1 small red onion, finely sliced
1 tbsp white wine vinegar
3 tbsp extra virgin olive oil
1 green chilli, finely chopped
1 tsp caster sugar
½ tsp sea salt
¼ tsp freshly ground black pepper
175g okra
1 tomato (110g), sliced

For the crumb:
1 tbsp olive oil
5 tbsp panko breadcrumbs
   or normal breadcrumbs
Sea salt and freshly ground
   black pepper

SERVES:
2
PREP:
10 MINS,
PLUS
15 MINS
MARINATING
COOK:
5 MINS

· Mix the sliced onion, vinegar, olive oil, chilli, sugar, salt and pepper in a bowl. Leave to marinate for 15 minutes.

· Wash and pat dry the okra with kitchen paper. Steam them over boiling water for 5 minutes, until slightly tender but still retaining a bite.

· Meanwhile, heat a small frying pan over a medium-high heat and add the olive oil and breadcrumbs. Toss them well together for around 2 minutes until golden brown. Season with salt and pepper.

· Once the okra is cooked it will be vibrant green in colour. Take it out of the steamer and cut off and discard the top hard ends. Slice the okra into 2cm pieces. Place in a medium-sized mixing bowl.

· Pour the onion marinade mixture over the okra and gently toss together. Add in the sliced tomato and gently mix. Scatter the breadcrumbs generously over the okra salad and serve immediately.

This is a refreshing Mauritian-style salad, combining juicy tomatoes (the riper the better), spicy chilli, crunchy red onion and a squeeze of lemon. Dressed with olive oil and fresh coriander, this salad frequents our family dinners on the island as it is so versatile and can be eaten with almost anything. It is perfect for spooning over Ginger & herb grilled red snapper (p.81), Grilled spiced lamb chops with lemon (p.60) or served alongside biryani and rice dishes.

RIPE TOMATO SALAD WITH CHILLI & LEMON
SATINI POMME D'AMOUR, MAURITIUS

5 ripe tomatoes (500g)
1 small red onion, finely chopped
Juice of ½ lemon
½ tsp sea salt

2–3 red chillies, finely chopped
2 tbsp olive oil
1 tbsp finely chopped coriander
Freshly ground black pepper

SERVES:
4–6
PREP:
20 MINS,
PLUS
15 MINS
CHILLING

· Cut the tomatoes in half, scoop out all the seeds from the middle and finely chop the tomato flesh (I take the seeds out because I find they can make the salad a little too watery).

· In a large bowl, combine all the remaining ingredients together with the tomatoes. Taste and season with pepper and more salt if needed. Cover and keep in the fridge for at least 15 minutes to allow the flavours to mingle.

· Keep the salad chilled until serving. It will keep in the fridge for 1 day if you want to make it ahead.

To me this salad represents the radiance of Mauritius, with its vibrant green spinach, ripe red tomatoes and luminous yellow-orange mango. It's an inviting bowl of fresh ingredients in its purest form, finished off with a glistening sweet-and-sour honey lime dressing that just dances in your mouth. It goes really well alongside grilled fish or chicken, or practically anything off the barbecue.

TOASTED COCONUT, MANGO & CARROT SALAD
MAURITIUS

50g freshly grated coconut (*see note on p.13*)

1 mango, peeled and cut into 1cm cubes (*see note on p.14*)

2 carrots, peeled and sliced into thin matchsticks

10 cherry tomatoes, quartered

50g spinach leaves, roughly chopped

Sea salt and freshly ground black pepper

For the dressing:

1 tsp honey

Juice of ½ lime

2 tbsp extra virgin olive oil

SERVES:
4

PREP:
15 MINS

· In a small bowl, mix together the dressing ingredients. Set aside.

· Toast the grated coconut in a pan over a medium heat until it starts to take on a little colour. Take out of the pan and set aside to cool.

· In a large bowl, toss together the mango and carrot matchsticks.

· Add the tomatoes to the bowl, together with the chopped spinach leaves. Sprinkle the salad with the toasted coconut, pepper and sea salt to taste. Drizzle with the dressing, toss the salad and add the juice from the remaining ½ lime if needed.

MALDIVES

FISH IS THE thing in the Maldives. For breakfast, lunch and dinner. How could it not be? These 1,190 islands – only 185 of them inhabited – are surrounded by ocean. Glorious pale blue waters rendered almost luminescent by the white sand that lies below their surface make up ninety-nine per cent of this tiny republic. And the king of fish here is tuna. Four different varieties are landed: yellow fin, little tunny, skipjack and frigate.

Before there were any visitors to the Maldives – be they conquerors, explorers or tourists staying in luxurious resorts – there were just fish, coconuts, yams, mangoes, papayas and pineapples. But as people criss-crossed the oceans in search of spices and adventure, some lingered on these twenty-six atolls, introducing the local palate to the ingredients they brought in their bags: chillies, spices, curry leaves. Others came to trade, leaving with holds stuffed with dried fish and coconuts which had been bartered in exchange for cardamom and turmeric and other treats. The fondness for 'short eats' found across many Indian Ocean islands is a ritual here, where they're known as *hedhikaa* and are a combination of fried savoury snacks and sweet treats, most often eaten around 4pm. *Bis keemiya* is my favourite *hedhikaa*: a pastry parcel stuffed with gently sautéed, shredded cabbage, hard-boiled eggs and spiced onions.

All across the Maldives you'll see – and of course smell – locals cooking in the old way on a *dhumashi*,

where a grill is placed over burning coconut shells and husks, which impart a fragrant smoke into fresh fish or a big pot of curry.

The Maldives literally means the islands (*dives*) of Malé, which is the capital city and the name of the largest island. At the vegetable and fruit market here, traders scribble prices on worn notepads as they pitch their bounty of vast watermelons grown on surrounding atolls, red and green 'Githeyo mirus' chillies, Chinese salad leaves holding droplets of dew, purple conical-shaped banana flowers and the unusual screwpine, a large green fruit, that when cut into sections reveals an alluring red-peachy hue. The fresh and dried fish market is an absolute must – you'll see enormous, shiny tuna being cut into steaks as well as shelves stacked with sun-dried, smoked tuna slices (known as 'Maldive fish') which are preferred by insistent stall-holders.

Family get-togethers happen almost weekly in the Maldives. The majority population is Muslim and so generations gather after Friday prayers for a feast before the weekend. If you're lucky enough to be invited as a guest, you might find tables laid with dishes such as *dhon riha*, a typical tuna curry where the fish is lusciously coated in aromatic fennel, black pepper, chillies, curry leaves and coconut milk – to be soaked up with *roshi*, sautéed Chinese leaves or banana flowers. The meal might end with *dhonkeyo kajuru*, crisp banana fritters with vanilla – and a nap in a hammock.

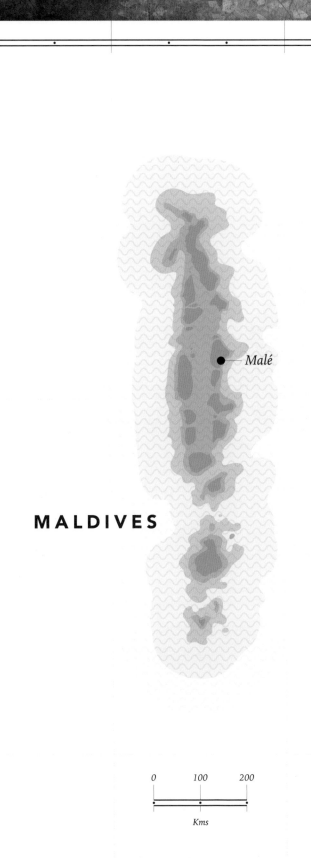

Malé

MALDIVES

0   100   200

Kms

My aunt Mila would make this dish when we came to visit her in Vacoa (my mother's hometown), located in the centre of Mauritius. It's a reviving broth of healthy greens, spiked with pungent garlic and warming ginger. I've found it a joy to watch her cooking since I was a child; she'd be crying with laughter from the start of slicing the onions to the final stirring of the pot of withered greens. We would have this as a starter before eating our meal, or enjoy a few spoonfuls over some rice.

I have used watercress and pak choi, but you can use a different combination of greens – Chinese leaves, spring greens or spinach would all work well.

WATERCRESS & PAK CHOI BROTH
BOUILLON CRESSON, MAURITIUS

100g watercress
1 pak choi
2 tbsp vegetable oil
1 onion, thinly sliced
2.5cm piece of fresh root ginger, peeled and grated

2 garlic cloves, finely chopped
1 small tomato, chopped
750ml vegetable stock
Sea salt and freshly ground black pepper

SERVES:
2
PREP:
10 MINS
COOK:
10 MINS

· Wash the watercress and pak choi in a colander to remove any dirt or impurities and pat dry with kitchen paper. Chop the watercress into 5cm pieces and set aside. Cut a slice off the base of the pak choi and chop the stalk into small chunks. Keep the stalks and leaves separate as they will cook at different times.

· In a deep saucepan over a medium-high heat, add the vegetable oil and gently fry the sliced onion for 2–3 minutes until translucent. Add in the ginger, garlic and tomato and cook for another 2 minutes, stirring occasionally. Pour in the vegetable stock and turn the heat down to a medium simmer. Add in the pak choi stalks and cook for 5 minutes. Check for seasoning and add salt or pepper if needed and then the pak choi leaves to gently wilt.

· Divide the watercress into serving bowls and pour the soup over until it's just submerged – the residual heat will cook the greens just enough. Alternatively, ladle over steamed basmati rice with some chilli sauce on the side.

The flavours in this heartwarming soup are a match made in the tropics. The cayenne pepper offers a pleasing heat, the ginger adds a note of spice and the coconut milk lends a mellow creaminess, but it is the sweet potato that's the star of the show. This starchy tuber is a particularly important crop in Comoros; the island's native potatoes are 'Katuna' (with red skin and yellow flesh) and 'Zora' (with yellow skin and white flesh). They are boiled, mashed, fried and ground into a flour to make cakes and even used to break fasting during the religious month of Ramadan.

Don't miss out the lime wheel at the end; this flash of sharp citrus complements the natural sweetness of the potato.

CREAMY SWEET POTATO SOUP
COMOROS & MAYOTTE

2 tbsp coconut oil
1 onion, diced
2 garlic cloves, finely chopped
2.5cm piece of fresh root ginger, peeled and finely grated
2 large sweet potatoes, peeled and cut into 4cm chunks (550g)
1 large ripe tomato, roughly chopped
¼ tsp cayenne pepper

1 tsp sea salt
Freshly ground black pepper
200ml coconut milk

To serve:
1 lime, cut into thin wheels or wedges
Mint and coriander leaves

SERVES:
4 AS A STARTER, 2 AS A MAIN
PREP:
10 MINS
COOK:
25 MINS

· Heat the coconut oil in a deep saucepan over a medium heat and fry the diced onion and garlic together in the pan for 5 minutes, stirring frequently to prevent them sticking to the bottom.

· Add the grated ginger, sweet potato, tomato, cayenne pepper, salt and some black pepper. Give it a good stir to ensure everything is mixed well. Pour in 500ml water, bring to the boil, then cover with the lid and let this simmer for 15–20 minutes until the sweet potato is soft and tender.

· Place the contents of the saucepan in a blender and whiz until smooth. Pour back into the saucepan on a low simmer, add in 150ml of the coconut milk and stir gently. Check for seasoning to see if more salt or pepper is needed.

· Serve the soup in bowls, with a drizzle of the remaining coconut milk, laying a few of the lime wheels on top of the soup. Scatter over mint and coriander leaves to garnish. Serve with some crusty bread.

A bowl of pure, wholesome, warming goodness. The combination of aubergine, chickpeas and sweet coconut milk makes this 'cari' divine, tumbled over steamed white rice, with some Island-style rotis (p.138) to scoop up leftover sauce.

I have used 'Kala chana' – these are small, dark-brown chickpeas with a nutty flavour. They can be sourced in Asian stores either tinned or dried in packets. If you cannot find them you can use a tin of normal chickpeas.

SEYCHELLOIS AUBERGINE & CHICKPEA CARI
SEYCHELLES

1 aubergine, chopped into 3cm cubes
3 tbsp olive oil
1 onion, finely chopped
6 curry leaves, fresh or dried, finely chopped
2 green chillies, finely sliced
2 garlic cloves, finely chopped
1 tomato, roughly chopped
1 tsp ground turmeric
1 tbsp Seychellois *massalé* (p.98) or mild curry powder

1 cinnamon stick or 1 tsp ground cinnamon
400ml tin coconut milk
2 medium potatoes, peeled and cut into large chunks
400g tin 'Kala chana' chickpeas, drained
1 tbsp chopped parsley
Sea salt and freshly ground black pepper
1 lime, cut into wedges, to serve

SERVES:
4
PREP:
20 MINS, PLUS 15 MINS SALTING
COOK:
40–50 MINS

- First mix the chopped aubergine in a bowl with 1 teaspoon salt and leave for 15 minutes, then pat dry with kitchen paper.

- Add 2 tablespoons of the oil to a frying pan over a high heat, and tip in the aubergine. Fry for 6–8 minutes, until golden brown on all sides. You can do this in batches so they all cook evenly. Set aside.

- Add the remaining 1 tablespoon of oil to a large saucepan over a medium heat and fry the onion, curry leaves, chilli and garlic together for a couple of minutes until the onions have softened slightly, stirring occasionally to avoid any sticking at the bottom of the pan. Next add in the tomato and cook for 2 minutes more until it starts to break down into the sauce.

- Sprinkle in the turmeric, *massalé* or curry powder and cinnamon, and stir well into the onion and tomato mixture, which will turn a bright yellow.

- Deglaze the pan with 50ml water, stirring frequently to lift up any bits sticking to the pan. Add in the coconut milk, potato and ½ teaspoon salt. Lower the heat and let this simmer for 15 minutes before adding in the chickpeas and fried aubergine and cooking for a further 5 minutes.

- Check the potato is tender and taste for seasoning. Sprinkle over black pepper and parsley and serve with lime wedges.

I see this comforting dish as Réunion's version of mac 'n' cheese – you'll sigh with joy after the first bite. Instead of pasta, it features a pear-shaped fruit that goes by many names – chou chou, christophine or chayote – whose flesh tastes similar to courgette and works particularly well with the sweetness of the pumpkin. You can find chou chou (chayote) in Asian grocers or use courgette or squash as a substitute.

The crunchy breadcrumb topping adds extra bite, before the silky, creamy sauce beneath takes over. Serve alongside grilled meats or chicken or eat as it is with some green vegetables.

PUMPKIN & CHOU CHOU GRATIN
GRATIN DE CHOU CHOU, RÉUNION

2 tbsp olive oil
1 onion, finely diced
600g pumpkin or squash, peeled and cut into 2cm cubes
1 large chou chou (chayote) (425g), peeled and cut into 2cm cubes (*see note opposite*)
3 thyme sprigs, leaves picked
1 garlic clove, finely chopped
¼ tsp cayenne pepper
¼ tsp caster sugar

Sea salt and freshly ground black pepper

For the béchamel sauce:
30g butter
30g plain flour
300ml whole milk
75g Gruyère (or Cheddar) cheese, grated
¼ tsp ground nutmeg
20g breadcrumbs (I used panko breadcrumbs, but any will do)

SERVES:
4
PREP:
20 MINS
COOK:
1 HOUR

· Preheat the oven to 210°C/Fan 190°C/Gas 7.

· Place a large, shallow saucepan over a medium heat. Add the olive oil and gently cook the onion for 5–7 minutes until slightly softened. Add in the pumpkin and chou chou (chayote), and give this a good stir. Next scatter in the thyme, garlic, cayenne and sugar and season with ½ teaspoon salt and some pepper. Sauté for 5 minutes. Pour in 50ml water, cover, turn down to a low simmer and cook for 25–35 minutes, or until the pumpkin and chayote are soft and tender.

· While this is cooking, make the béchamel sauce. In a small saucepan, melt the butter over a medium heat. Add in the flour and whisk together. The mixture will start to clump and slowly turn a light brown colour. Cook for around 2 minutes, stirring continuously, and pour in the milk a little bit at a time while whisking continuously, until all the milk is added. Gradually bring the mixture to the boil, then reduce the heat and simmer for 2 minutes, until thickened.

- Remove from the heat, add 50g of the Gruyère and the nutmeg and whisk until all the cheese has melted and the sauce is luscious, silky and smooth. Season and set aside.

- Take the pumpkin and chou chou off the heat when cooked and, using the back of a fork, mash roughly so there are only slight lumps (I like this for texture, but you can mash it smoother if you prefer).

- Put the mixture into a 22cm gratin dish and gently flatten out with the back of a spoon. Spoon the cheesy béchamel sauce over the pumpkin and chou chou mash until it's completely covered. Scatter the remaining 25g cheese and breadcrumbs on top. Bake in the oven for 20 minutes until golden and bubbling.

Peeling chou chou (chayote)

- When peeling chou chou, rub your hands with a little oil. This will help them not to get sticky with the liquid from the vegetable while preparing. Peel the green skin with a potato peeler or knife, cut in half to remove the hard core, then chop the flesh.

'Touffé' is a braising technique in Mauritius, where the vegetables are sautéed with onions, garlic, ginger, thyme and chilli, then steamed with a little water. This method of cooking makes the potatoes turn almost creamy and intensifies the flavour of the vegetables. My mum would make this at home quite often when she needed to cook something quickly; sometimes using shredded cabbage ('touffé lisou'). It's traditionally served as a side dish to something like 'poisson salé' (salt fish) in a chilli sauce, but it also pairs well with the Sausages in spicy tomato sauce (p.54).

BRAISED AUBERGINE WITH POTATOES & CHILLI
TOUFFÉ BRINGEL, MAURITIUS

1 aubergine (200g), ends removed, sliced into chunks
2 tbsp olive oil
1 red onion, sliced
2 medium potatoes (260g), peeled and cut into quarters
2 garlic cloves, finely chopped
2.5cm piece of fresh root ginger, peeled and finely chopped

4 thyme sprigs, leaves picked
1 red chilli, seeds in, finely chopped
2 tomatoes (140g), chopped
1 tsp tomato purée
Small pinch of caster sugar
Sea salt and freshly ground black pepper
Small handful of coriander leaves, to serve

SERVES:
2
PREP:
20 MINS, PLUS 15 MINS SALTING
COOK:
30 MINS

· Place your aubergine chunks in a small mixing bowl and sprinkle with salt. Leave for 15 minutes to draw out any extra moisture and bitterness. Rinse and drain.

· Put a deep saucepan over a medium heat and add the olive oil. Sauté the sliced onion for a couple of minutes until it is translucent, then add in the potatoes. Tip in the garlic and ginger and give them a good mix. Cook for 5 minutes or so to brown slightly.

· Add in the aubergine, followed by the thyme, chilli, tomatoes, purée, pinch of sugar and ½ teaspoon salt and give it a good stir. Let the flavours mingle together for 2 minutes before pouring 200ml water into the pan so the potatoes and aubergine are slightly submerged.

· Cover with a lid and cook for 20 minutes over a medium heat, stirring if needed so it doesn't stick to the bottom of the pan. For the last 5 minutes, take the lid off until the sauce has reduced and intensified in flavour (this is a dry dish so there's not too much sauce). Check for seasoning and add more salt and black pepper if needed. Scatter over coriander for that uplifting freshness.

I first tried this dish in Cilaos, a forested, rugged caldera in Réunion. The area grows a tiny lentil called 'Lentille de Cilaos', a variety that is found only in these mountains with their fertile, volcanic soil, which lends the lentils a distinctive, earthy taste.

This dish was prepared by a young couple I met, Michel and Raymonda, who run a 'table d'hôte' (host's table) in the mountains. A cast-iron pot sat nestled in a smoking outdoor charcoal fire, and after cooking we sat to picnic on a bowl of these glossy, yellow-tinged turmeric lentils, aromatic with the homegrown herbs, piled on a mound of rice. This makes a filling vegetarian side dish or, like the Réunionese, you can add in some smoky sausages for a one-pot meal.

CREAMY LENTILS WITH THYME & TURMERIC
RÉUNION

250g green or brown lentils, rinsed
1 bay leaf
3 tbsp vegetable oil
1 large onion, finely sliced
4–5 thyme sprigs, leaves picked
2.5cm piece of fresh root ginger, peeled and finely chopped
2 garlic cloves, finely chopped

½ tsp ground turmeric
1 tsp ground cumin
1 tsp sea salt

To serve:
Natural yoghurt
2 tbsp chopped coriander

SERVES:
4 GENEROUSLY
PREP:
10 MINS
COOK:
35 MINS

· Place the lentils in a large deep saucepan, add 1 litre cold water, the bay leaf and bring to the boil over a high heat. Reduce the heat and simmer the lentils uncovered for 25 minutes. Add an extra 100ml cold water if the lentils absorb it all.

· In a medium frying pan, heat the vegetable oil to a medium heat. Add in the sliced onion and sauté for 5–7 minutes until softened. Next mix in the thyme, ginger and garlic and stir. Cook for 1 minute.

· Scatter in the turmeric and cumin. Mix well with the onions – they will turn a yellow-tinged colour and will be very aromatic. Fry for 30 seconds, stirring frequently. Take the pan off the heat and set aside.

· After 20–25 minutes' cooking the lentils should be tender. Add in the onion mixture and salt, stir well and cook for a further 10 minutes on a medium simmer. Using the back of a fork or a potato masher, gently press the lentils a little in the pan until they squish slightly and the texture becomes a bit more creamy. Check for seasoning.

· Serve immediately with a dollop of yoghurt and scattering of coriander.

This is a traditional Mauritian dish of beans and vegetables stewed in a tomato-based sauce flavoured with chillies. It's something you will find cooked in the homes of many Mauritians and it is less heavy than eating a curry – so one plate is never enough! The stew is light, fragrant with cinnamon and Provençale herbs, such as thyme, and the potatoes help to thicken the flavourful sauce. I love including the squash in here too; it adds sweetness amidst all that heat. This is great as a vegetarian meal served with some chutney, extra chillies and coconut rice (p.128).

KIDNEY BEAN, BUTTERNUT & POTATO STEW

LA DAUBE, MAURITIUS

2 tbsp vegetable oil
1 onion, finely chopped
2 garlic cloves, finely chopped
2.5cm piece of fresh root ginger, peeled and finely chopped
1 tsp paprika
1 tsp chilli powder or 1 chilli, finely chopped
4 thyme sprigs, leaves picked
1 small bunch of coriander, stalks and leaves separated and finely chopped

1 cinnamon stick or 1 tsp ground cinnamon
400g tin plum tomatoes
½ tsp salt
¼ tsp sugar
2 medium potatoes, peeled and cut into 3cm chunks
200g butternut squash, cut into 3cm cubes
400g tin kidney beans, drained
Sea salt and freshly ground black pepper

SERVES:
4
PREP:
15 MINS
COOK:
1 HOUR

- Put a deep saucepan over a medium heat, add the vegetable oil and cook the onion for 5–7 minutes until softened. Next add the garlic, ginger, paprika, chilli, thyme, coriander stalks and cinnamon, and stir to combine. Cook for 2 minutes, stirring frequently to avoid sticking.

- Tip in the plum tomatoes and salt, plus 150ml water. Using a wooden spoon, break down the tomatoes a little bit and add the sugar.

- Add in the potatoes, squash and kidney beans and mix gently so they are mostly submerged in the tomato sauce. Cover and simmer over a medium heat for 30 minutes. Uncover and simmer for a further 15–20 minutes, adding a little water if it becomes too dry.

- Check the potatoes and squash by piercing them with a fork – they should be soft. Remove and discard the cinnamon stick, if using. Check for seasoning, scatter with chopped coriander leaves and serve.

This is my mum's version of mashed potato: it amazes me that with only a few additional ingredients she transforms something plain into a dish with real Mauritian-style pizzazz. The fricassée of cooked onions, thyme leaves, garlic, tomato and chilli flakes, gently mixed into creamy potato, adds a bounty of taste. I eat this alongside a bowl of Watercress & pak choi broth (p.115), or Sausages in spicy tomato sauce (p.54).

MUM'S SPICY MASHED POTATO
SATINI POMME DE TERRE, MAURITIUS

3 medium potatoes (400g),
   peeled and cut into 3cm chunks
2 tbsp olive oil
1 onion, finely chopped
4 thyme sprigs, leaves picked
1 garlic clove, finely chopped

1 tomato (110g), seeds discarded
   and flesh roughly chopped
Generous pinch of chilli flakes
Sea salt and freshly ground
   black pepper
Small handful of coriander leaves,
   to serve

SERVES:
2–4
PREP:
10 MINS
COOK:
20 MINS

· Bring a large pan of water to the boil, add in ½ teaspoon sea salt and pop in the potatoes. Cook for around 20 minutes until tender and just falling apart.

· In the meantime, preheat a large frying pan to a medium heat, add the olive oil and sauté the onion for 5–7 minutes, until slightly softened. Add the thyme, garlic and tomato and cook for 2–3 minutes, stirring occasionally. Sprinkle in a pinch of chilli flakes, then set aside.

· Drain the potatoes using a colander and mash them with a potato masher in the same pan. Once it is smooth, with no lumps, tip the mashed potato into the cooked onion mixture. Using a spoon, gently mix it well together so the onion runs through the mashed potato. Season with salt and pepper and serve with a scattering of coriander leaves.

Narrow rice paddies are carved into hills and valleys throughout Madagascar. After fertilising the sown rice, old traditions are kept alive in many villages, with families and neighbours joining together in a festive trampling of the fields with their cattle. It is a real community event, protecting their livelihood. Rice, called 'vary' in Madagascar, is eaten three times a day, as 'potage' (porridge) for breakfast, for lunch and dinner, so it is vitally important, which is why there are many varieties on this island alone. One of them is the highly sought-after 'pink rice', with its subtle tropical notes of cinnamon, cloves and nutmeg. Pink rice can be sourced online.

Coconut rice is a dish common in the coastal areas of Madagascar, where the coconut trees are abundant and so coconuts are affordable for people to buy. The coconut milk lends the rice a creamy texture, so it's a little sticky and indulgent, calling for a robust partner. This tastes particularly great with the Sticky chicken with garlic & ginger (p.27).

MALAGASY COCONUT RICE
VARY AMIN'NY VOANIO, MADAGASCAR

150g basmati or jasmine rice
1 cinnamon stick
½ tsp sea salt
200ml coconut milk

2 tbsp coconut oil
1 onion, sliced
10 curry leaves, fresh or dried

SERVES:
2–3
PREP:
15 MINS,
PLUS
30 MINS
SOAKING
COOK:
25 MINS

· Firstly soak the rice for 30 minutes in cold water (or wash a few times until the water runs clear). Drain well.

· In a deep saucepan over a medium heat, add the rice, cinnamon stick, salt, coconut milk and 50ml water. Bring to the boil, then turn down to a simmer. Cook for 10 minutes until the water has evaporated. Using a fork, fluff up the rice, cover and set aside to steam for 5 minutes.

· In a separate frying pan over a medium heat, add the coconut oil then tip in the sliced onion and sauté for 2–3 minutes, until it goes slightly brown around the edges. Scatter in the curry leaves and continue frying the onion for 4 minutes until charred brown and a little crisp. Once cooked, liberally scatter the onion over the coconut rice and run a fork through everything to gently mix.

For me, rice is an empty canvas waiting to be experimented with. When I had this dish in a local guesthouse in Mahé, I marvelled at its vibrant colours: it was bright with sweet, crunchy peppers and fresh herbs, and gorgeously aromatic with spices. 'Saffran' is the Creole term for the spice turmeric, which is freshly grated into the rice or ground and then added to give it a beautiful colour. This is eaten alongside a fragrant dish like the King prawns with tamarind & coconut (p.98).

Basmati rice, with its slender grains, is perfect for this dish; however, you can use jasmine as an alternative. Always soak or wash the rice grains first in cold water until the water runs clear. This will get rid of any impurities and make the rice much fluffier when cooked.

CREOLE SAFFRAN RICE
SEYCHELLES

200g basmati rice
2 tbsp olive oil
1 large shallot or small onion,
   finely chopped
2 garlic cloves, finely chopped
2.5cm piece of fresh root ginger,
   peeled and finely chopped

5 curry leaves, fresh or dried
1 red pepper, diced
1 tsp ground turmeric
½ tsp ground cinnamon
2 tbsp chopped parsley
Sea salt and freshly ground
   black pepper

SERVES:
4
PREP:
10 MINS,
PLUS
30 MINS
SOAKING
COOK:
20 MINS

- Firstly soak the rice for 30 minutes in cold water (or wash a few times until the water runs clear). Drain well. Cook your rice in accordance with the packet instructions.

- Meanwhile, heat the olive oil in a medium saucepan over a medium heat. Fry the shallot or onion with the garlic, ginger and curry leaves for 5–7 minutes, stirring occasionally.

- Add in the diced red pepper and ½ teaspoon sea salt and cook for 2–3 minutes, until slightly softened but still retaining its crunch. Sprinkle over the turmeric and cinnamon and mix well into the ingredients.

- When the rice is cooked, stir it into the shallot mixture until it is yellow all over. Sprinkle over salt and pepper to season and scatter over the parsley leaves. Give it one more gentle mix and spoon onto a platter to serve.

'Riz frit' (stir-fried rice) is a Chinese-inspired dish introduced when immigrants came to work and settle in Mauritius, quickly establishing a Chinatown in the capital Port Louis. Most were traders and merchants and their cuisine became ingrained into Mauritian culture – we now have dishes like Sunny-side-up egg, chicken & pak choi rice bowl (p.28) and fried noodles and dumplings, which can be found across the island.

This is the traditional combination of vegetables used in fried rice, but you can always add alternatives – fresh or frozen peas and sweetcorn work well. The fish sauce adds a depth of umami to the dish and those slices of omelette make it a hearty dinner. You can use leftover rice for this; just make sure it has been chilled after cooking. This works well as a main dish served with a Ripe tomato salad with chilli & lemon (p.109) and some red chilli sauce, or it can also be eaten as a side.

MAURITIAN FRIED RICE WITH VEGETABLES
RIZ FRIT, MAURITIUS

150g basmati rice
1 tbsp sesame oil
3 eggs, beaten
2 tbsp vegetable oil
1 onion, finely chopped
1 garlic clove, finely chopped
1 green chilli, finely chopped
1 carrot, peeled and chopped
    into fine batons

50g green beans
70g white cabbage, finely sliced
2 tbsp dark or light soy sauce
1 tbsp fish sauce (optional)
1 tbsp finely chopped chives
2 spring onions, finely chopped
1 tbsp chopped coriander

SERVES:
3–4
PREP:
15 MINS,
PLUS
30 MINS
SOAKING
COOK:
30 MINS

· Firstly soak the rice for 30 minutes in cold water (or wash a few times until the water runs clear). Drain well. Cook your rice in accordance with the packet instructions.

· Meanwhile, prepare all your other ingredients and lay them out on a plate, so you are ready to cook fast when the time comes.

· To make the omelette, bring a non-stick frying pan to a medium-high heat on the hob, add the sesame oil and pour in the beaten eggs. Let them cook for 2–3 minutes before gently lifting up to check underneath: the omelette

should be a nice golden yellow colour. Using a spatula, flip the omelette over. Cook on the other side for 1–2 minutes and slide off onto a plate. Cut the omelette up into strips and leave to cool slightly.

· Next preheat a wok to a medium-high heat. Pour in the vegetable oil and add in the onion, garlic and chilli. Fry this for 2 minutes, frequently stirring. Working quickly, add in the carrot, green beans and white cabbage. Sprinkle in the soy sauce and fish sauce (if using) and coat the vegetables well. Cook for 2–3 minutes until the veg are softened but still retain a slight crunch.

· Add in the cooked rice and mix well with the vegetables. Let this cook for 2 minutes more. Spoon the fried rice onto a serving plate or platter and scatter over the omelette strips, chives, spring onion and coriander to finish. Serve immediately with chilli sauce, pickles or chutney.

SEYCHELLES

GINGER, LEMONGRASS, CORIANDER AND TAMARIND – these are the ingredients that make Seychellois cuisine sing. Fish is, of course, the cornerstone of cooking here, since the more-than forty inner islands are surrounded by pristine ocean. It's eaten almost every day of the week except Sunday – when families sometimes push the boat out and have chicken, beef or pork. You'll find tuna, bonito, dorado, kingfish (also known as wahoo), marlin, mackerel, squid, crab – and parrotfish, which is used to make a Creole fish and chips.

They eat shark here – I know the idea makes many people squeamish. I've tried it in a chutney known as *satini reken*, where the skinned shark is finely mashed, and cooked with squeezed *bilimbi* (a small sour cucumber) juice and mixed with onion, pepper, salt and turmeric. I've not included a recipe – don't worry. And I'm not giving one for bat curry, another local predilection which, like many foods in the world, came from the needs-must tradition.

Like its Indian Ocean neighbours, the Seychelles have been shaped by colonialists bringing their own appetites along with poor slaves from nearby Madagascar and many other parts of Africa. The influence of the French is right there in *bouillon tec tec*: this is a broth made from little local clams, flavoured with wine like *moules marinières*. The 115 islands of the Seychelles are so remote that they were undiscovered until the French plonked their flag on the sand in 1756. But in spite of this Gallic hinterland, the cooking is very definitely Creole with influences of African, Chinese and even British cooking.

The Seychellois love hot chillies; there are ten local varieties and there's a pot of them on every table. This thirst for fire means that a Seychellois curry is *hot*. Rice is most often the accompaniment, closely followed by breadfruit – look at the trees around you and you'll notice that many have branches burgeoning with these green prickly globes. I love the breadfruit chips made here, which are salty and addictive.

The fruit on the Seychelles is reverie-inducing – pineapple, soursop, papaya, custard apples and jackfruit are my favourites, sold on roadside stalls. It's a good idea to pop a small penknife into your suitcase so that you can cut up fruit as you fancy it across the Indian Ocean islands.

The rich smell of spices fills the air of the Seychelles – and nowhere more than in the Jardin du Roi, a haven of nature in the hills above Anse Royale where vanilla, cinnamon, citronella and nutmeg grow. I ponder the story of Pierre Poivre, the French horticulturalist and botanist who clandestinely smuggled plants and sowed them here. When I'm cooking Seychellois recipes, it's hard not to sing 'Peter Pepper stole some pepper' because his smuggling brought such incredible flavours to these islands.

PRASLIN

LA DIGUE

SEYCHELLES
(INNER ISLANDS)

SILHOUETTE

Victoria

MAHÉ

Anse Royale

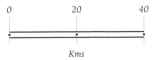

0   20   40

Kms

I visited chef Christelle Verheyden at La Grande Maison restaurant, located next to the Takamaka rum distillery in Au Cap on the east coast of the Seychelles. Housed in an old colonial-style building, it remains a historically important settlement with a long association with farming tropical spices, which are blended into Takamaka rums.

Christelle has a gift for combining these spices in her menus; I tried her famous French-Creole bouillabaisse, a soup made from freshwater fish, a spoonful of rouille and served with 'carrypile' (curry leaf) rolls. It was the bread that had me wanting more. The taste was unbelievable: soft, fluffy little rolls with a golden sheen, and aromatic curry leaves baked inside each one.

In my version I have added in turmeric and cumin seeds for earthy, nutty undertones and finely chopped the curry leaves so they are dispersed through the rolls for flavour in every bite. These should be eaten warm from the oven with a smear of butter alongside your main meal, or are great stuffed with Spicy lamb patties (p.169), drizzled with yoghurt.

CURRY LEAF BREAD ROLLS
SEYCHELLES

250g strong white bread flour,
  plus extra for kneading
2 tbsp finely chopped curry leaves
½ tsp ground turmeric
½ tsp cumin seeds, slightly crushed

Pinch of caster sugar
1 tsp sea salt
1 x 7g sachet fast-acting yeast
150ml warm water

MAKES:
6–10 ROLLS
PREP:
15 MINS,
PLUS
1 HOUR
PROVING
COOK:
20 MINS

· Sift the white bread flour into a large mixing bowl. Add the curry leaves, turmeric, cumin seeds, sugar and salt. Mix well to combine, then sprinkle in the fast-action yeast.

· Make a well in the middle of the flour and pour in the water slowly while mixing together to create a dough. Place the dough on a floured clean work surface and knead for 10 minutes. Use the heel of your hand to push the dough away from you then back again, and continue to do this until it is soft, smooth and pliable.

· Portion the dough into six small pieces (or ten to make mini rolls) and roll each into a ball. Place on a greased baking tray, about 5cm apart from each other.

· Cover the rolls with a damp tea towel or greased cling film and leave to prove in a warm place for 1 hour until they have doubled in size.

· Preheat the oven to 210°C/Fan 190°C/Gas 7.

· Remove the cling film or tea towel and place the proved bread rolls in the oven for 15–20 minutes (or 7–10 minutes for the smaller ones) until golden brown. Serve warm from the oven, generously buttered.

'Rotis', also known as 'farata' and 'paratha', are a favourite street food in Mauritius. These flatbreads were a must on our family dinner table; I would stand near the hot stove watching my mother flipping them on the hot 'tawa' (flat pan) while they puffed up. I love these soft, fluffy breads, with their slightly charred flavour where the brown spots appear. We would eat them with a good smear of butter, or served with a chicken, lamb, beef or fish 'cari'.

By using the folding and oiling method, you get more flaky crusts and buttery layers in the 'roti' to soak up the sauces. To keep them from going hard after cooking, wrap them in a clean tea towel inside a large bowl until they are ready to be eaten.

ISLAND-STYLE ROTIS
ALL ISLANDS

300g plain white flour, plus extra
  for kneading
1 tsp sea salt
3 tbsp vegetable oil, plus extra for
  brushing and frying

140ml hot water, or enough
  to make a dough

MAKES:
6 ROTIS
PREP:
10 MINS,
PLUS
30 MINS
RESTING
COOK:
15 MINS

· Sift the flour and salt into a large bowl. Pour in the oil and gently mix with your fingers or a wooden spoon until the oil has been incorporated into the flour. Pour in enough hot water to make a soft, but not sticky, dough, adding a little more flour or water if needed to get the right consistency. Tip the dough onto a lightly floured surface and knead gently for 5 minutes until pliable and smooth. Cover with a damp tea towel and leave to rest for around 30 minutes.

· Divide the dough into six equal pieces and roll each one into a thin circle about the thickness of a 5-pence coin, using a rolling pin.

· Lightly brush the *roti* with oil using a pastry brush, and fold into a square by joining the top and the bottom together and then the other sides together onto the previous fold. Repeat with the remaining five *roti*. Leave to rest.

· Heat a little oil in a heavy-based pan or crêpe pan over a medium-high heat. Roll one of the *roti* into a square (about the thickness of a 5-pence coin) with a rolling pin, and cook on one side for 2–3 minutes or until it puffs up and is speckled light brown on the underside. Turn it over and fry on the other side for 1½–2 minutes until it too is puffed up. Remove from the pan, cool slightly and fold into four. Wrap in a clean tea towel placed on a plate or in a large bowl. Cook the remaining *rotis* in the same way and serve warm.

SNACKS
AND
STREET FOOD

Spicy Bread Fritters with Chilli & Tomato
MOFO SAKAY, MADAGASCAR

Potato & Pea Samosas
MAURITIUS

Golden Egg & White Cabbage Pastries
BIS KEEMIYA, MALDIVES

Lonumirus Spiced Fried Fish
THELULI MAS, MALDIVES

Breadfruit Chips with Paprika & Sea Salt
SEYCHELLES

Chilli Dhal Fritters
GATEAUX PIMENTS, MAURITIUS

Cumin & Lentil Flatbreads
DHAL PURI, MAURITIUS

Stuffed Peppers with Sardines & Chilli
PIMENT FARCI, MAURITIUS

Grilled Beef Skewers with Peanut Sauce
MASIKITA, MADAGASCAR

Spicy Lamb Patties
CATLESS, MAURITIUS

Pork Dumplings with Soy Ginger Dip
BOUCHONS, RÉUNION

Chilli Prawn Fritters
CREVETTES CROUSTILLANTES, MAURITIUS

Tuna & Coconut Flatbreads
MASROSHI, MALDIVES

Sardine Croquettes
BOULETTES SARDINE, MAURITIUS

SNACKS
AND
STREET FOOD

THANKS TO THE exciting mix of ethnicities across the islands – Indian, French, Creole, African and Chinese – the shared culture of street food is hard to beat, from the *gajacks* of Mauritius to the *hedhikaa* of the Maldives. Locals will always make time to head to their favourite vendor selling hot, fresh snacks or Creole-style tapas, and these can be found on the beaches, at the roadside, on market stalls, even on the backs of mopeds, where delicious morsels are transported around in containers along with any extras, from chilli sauce to fresh chutneys. It's normal to buy a selection of different snacks to try a few at a time.

The Indian-influenced samosa, called *sambosa* in Madagascar, can be found throughout all of these islands with a variety of fillings, depending on where they are made. One of my favourites is stuffed with pea and potato with hints of spice (p.146), but you'll also find tuna with red chilli in the Seychelles and minced beef samosas in Madagascar. Further cultural crossover is provided by the popular snack *bis keemiya* (Golden egg & white cabbage pastries, p.150), a mix between a samosa and spring roll from the Maldives, which marries together the Indian and Chinese versions. Most of these delights are fried for that irresistible crispy crust and if it's something crunchy and

golden you are after to enjoy with a cold drink, you can't find better than *gateaux piments* (p.156), chilli and lentil fritters that are famous throughout Mauritius. However, not all the recipes in this chapter are fried – you'll also find Grilled beef skewers with peanut sauce from Madagascar (p.164), steamed dumplings (p.170) and Stuffed peppers with sardines & chilli (p.163).

Spicy, colourful and varied, the recipes here provide delectable bursts of flavour that are impossible to resist, from vegetarian fritters, samosas and breads to crispy fried fish and pork dumplings. For the full 'island experience', serve them with a freshly blended chilli sauce or one of the chutneys and pickles on pp.185–197.

'Mofo sakay', which translates as 'spicy bread', is a much-loved Malagasy treat sold from street food stalls. Generous spoonfuls of batter flavoured with chopped chillies, tomato and watercress are deep fried in hot oil. The resulting peppery fritters are crisp outside and pillowy-soft inside. Serve them piled on a plate, ready to share, with a small bowl of Hot chilli dipping sauce (p.196) or Green chilli paste with lemon (p.197) on the side.

SPICY BREAD FRITTERS WITH CHILLI & TOMATO
MOFO SAKAY, MADAGASCAR

200g plain flour, sifted
1 tsp sea salt
2 tsp mild curry powder
2 tsp baking powder
½ tsp freshly ground black pepper
4–5 green chillies, finely chopped

2 tomatoes (175g), seeds discarded and flesh finely chopped
1 small bunch of watercress (40g), finely chopped
1 litre vegetable oil, for deep frying

MAKES:
12 FRITTERS
PREP:
15 MINS
COOK:
LESS THAN
5 MINS
PER BATCH

· In a large mixing bowl, mix together the sifted flour, salt, curry powder, baking powder and black pepper and gradually whisk in 200ml water to create a smooth, thick batter, as lump free as possible. It should be thick enough to coat the back of a spoon and drip off slowly.

· Add the chopped chillies, tomatoes and watercress to the batter, ensuring the ingredients are all mixed together well.

· Heat the oil in a deep, heavy-based pan, or in a deep fat fryer if you have one, to 180°C or until a small piece of bread turns golden brown within 30 seconds of dropping it into the oil.

· Take heaped tablespoons of the batter and carefully drop or spoon them into the hot oil. Fry them in batches for 3–4 minutes, until the fritters are golden brown and cooked throughout. Use a fork or a slotted spoon to flip them over to get them evenly brown all over.

· Remove the fritters with a slotted spoon and place onto a wire rack with kitchen paper underneath to catch any excess oil (this will help the fritters stay nice and crispy). Pile onto a plate and serve with a chilli sauce or paste to dip.

The moment I land in Mauritius, my first craving is for samosas. We buy a whole brown paper bagful to nibble on as we drive along the winding coastal roads back to our family home. Slightly smaller in size than the samosas you may know, they are a perfect one- (or two-!) bite snack, filled with chilli, spiced potato and peas, which give delicious bursts of sweetness. You may find these are spicy enough and you don't need chutney, but they do go well with the Coriander green chilli chutney (p.190) or Sweet mango & red chilli chutney (p.194).

I have chosen to bake these samosas instead of fry them as they are less greasy this way and you still get that delicious crunch. You can buy the samosa or spring roll pastry sheets from the fresh or frozen sections in Asian stores or large supermarkets. Leftover sheets can be stored in the freezer for next time.

POTATO & PEA SAMOSAS
MAURITIUS

1½ tsp salt

3 medium potatoes (500g),
  peeled and cut into 1cm cubes

2 tbsp olive oil

1 onion, finely chopped

2 garlic cloves, finely chopped

2.5cm piece of fresh root ginger,
  peeled and finely chopped

5 curry leaves, fresh or dried,
  finely chopped

3 thyme sprigs, leaves picked

1 red or green chilli, finely chopped

1 tbsp medium curry powder

70g green peas (fresh or frozen)

½ tsp ground cumin

1 tbsp finely chopped coriander

7 spring roll or samosa pastry sheets
  (25cm square)

1 egg, beaten

1 tbsp sesame seeds

MAKES:
21 SAMOSAS

PREP:
50 MINS

COOK:
1 HOUR

- In a large, deep saucepan filled with boiling water and 1 teaspoon of the salt, boil the potato cubes until just tender, around 15 minutes. Drain and leave to cool slightly, then cut them into even smaller cubes, around 5mm.

- Add the oil to a large frying pan over a medium heat. Cook the onion until softened and translucent, around 5–7 minutes. Add in the garlic, ginger, curry leaves, thyme and chilli and fry for a further 2 minutes.

- Scatter over the curry powder, potatoes, peas, cumin and the remaining ½ teaspoon of salt and mix well together so the potatoes are a lovely yellow colour, coated in the spices.

- Cook the mixture over a low heat for 5 minutes, adding a splash of water if it gets too dry. Set aside to cool and mix in the coriander.

- Preheat the oven to 200°C/Fan 180°C/Gas 6.

- Unwrap the pastry and take out one sheet, covering the rest with cling film or a damp cloth to stop them from drying out.

- Lay the sheet out on a clean work surface and, using a knife, cut it into three strips of equal size lengthways (about 8cm in width).

- Take a scant 2 tablespoons of the potato and pea mixture and place on the bottom right hand corner of the strip on the side closest to you. Take this corner and fold over the filling diagonally into the shape of a triangle. Dab some of the beaten egg along the edge to seal the filling in the samosa, proceeding to do this all the way to the top. Again, seal the edges and lightly brush each triangle all over with egg.

- Sprinkle over the sesame seeds and place the samosas on to two baking trays lined with baking parchment. Put them in the oven for 30 minutes until golden brown and crisp. Serve immediately.

Variations

- Once you have got used to the technique of samosa making, you can experiment with fillings: flaked tuna with chilli; a cheese like mozzarella with finely chopped fresh herbs; or sautéed beef or lamb mince flecked with curry spices.

Pictured overleaf

These crispy pastries filled with shredded cabbage, boiled egg, onion, chilli and curry leaves are one of the classic Maldivian 'short eats' or snacks – somewhere between a samosa and a spring roll. I first tasted them at the Lagoon Beach Café for 'hedhikaa' (Maldivian afternoon tea). A large container filled with freshly fried spicy treats was brought to our beachside table, brimming with 'gulha' (smoked tuna and coconut balls), 'bajiya' (triangle pastries filled with tuna and caramelised onions) and – my favourite – the crisp 'bis keemiya'. They are traditionally enjoyed with strong, black Sri Lankan tea. The pastries are usually made with very spicy Maldivian 'Githeyo mirus' ('Scotch bonnet') chillies, which you can source online. I have chosen to bake these rather than fry them, and have added tuna to my version of the recipe, but you can omit this if you want to make them vegetarian.

GOLDEN EGG & WHITE CABBAGE PASTRIES
BIS KEEMIYA, MALDIVES

For the dough:
400g plain flour, sifted,
  plus extra for kneading
2 tbsp vegetable oil,
  plus extra for oiling
1 egg, beaten
1 tsp sea salt
150ml warm water
2 egg yolks, beaten, to glaze

For the filling:
2 tbsp vegetable oil

1 onion, finely chopped
10 curry leaves, fresh or dried,
  finely chopped
1 chilli ('Githeyo mirus'/
  'Scotch bonnet' or 'Habanero'),
  deseeded and finely chopped
200g white cabbage, finely sliced
120g tinned tuna,
  well-drained and flaked
1 tsp sea salt
1 tsp freshly ground black pepper
3 eggs, hard-boiled and chopped

MAKES: 12 PASTRIES
PREP: 45 MINS
COOK: 40 MINS

- Preheat the oven to 200°C/Fan 180°C/Gas 6.

- Firstly make the dough. Into a large mixing bowl add the sifted flour, vegetable oil, beaten egg and salt. Using your fingertips, mix the oil into the flour to give it a grainy, sand-like texture. Gradually add in just enough of the warm water to form a dough.

- Turn out onto a lightly floured surface and knead until smooth, around 5 minutes. (If it's too dry add a little more water and if it's too wet a little more flour until you reach the right texture.)

- Lightly smear the dough with a little oil, put into a clean bowl and cover the bowl in cling film. Leave to rest while making the filling.

- To make the filling, heat the vegetable oil in a large frying pan over a medium heat and sweat the onion, curry leaves and chilli together until the onion is translucent, around 5–7 minutes.

- Add in the sliced cabbage, tuna, salt and pepper and cook for 5 minutes or so, stirring frequently, until the cabbage has softened. Take off the heat and leave to cool. Stir through the chopped egg.

- To make the pastries, divide the rested dough into 12 golf-ball-sized pieces. Working one at a time, roll out into a 12–15cm disc. Place roughly 1 tablespoon of the filling in the centre and fold to enclose completely into the shape of a half moon, sealing the edges firmly (I use a fork to gently press the edges together, and you can add a touch of water around the rim to help it stick together). Place on two greaseproof-paper-lined baking trays.

- Brush the pastries with beaten yolk and add a sprinkling of salt. Bake for 25 minutes until golden. Serve warm.

'Theluli mas' means 'spicy fried fish' in the Maldivian language, Dhivehi. On the island of Hulhumalé in the North Malé Atoll in the Maldives, I was welcomed into the home of Soba to see how she cooked home-style dishes. I watched her make the traditional lonumirus spice paste for marinating the fish before it is fried – a punchy concoction of fresh coconut, red chillies, curry leaves and black peppercorns. Traditionally, she told me, they were ground with a 'funda dhaa', a large stone slab with a heavy cylindrical tool, but nowadays they use a pestle and mortar or blender. Sometimes 'Maldive fish' (cured, concentrated fish) is added to give a more pungent taste.

Usually made with tuna, this recipe also works with snapper, mackerel or freshwater fish such as trout. Leftover paste can be kept in the fridge to marinate other fish to cook on the grill or to be served as a condiment alongside curries or Fish soup with chilli & lime (p.69).

LONUMIRUS SPICED FRIED FISH
THELULI MAS, MALDIVES

2 tuna or snapper steaks (250g)
1 tsp tomato purée
Vegetable oil, for frying
Sea salt and freshly ground
   black pepper
1 lemon or lime, cut into wedges,
   to serve

For the spice paste:
1 tsp cumin seeds
10 dried red chillies
   or 'Kashmiri' red chillies

10 curry leaves
1 tsp whole black peppercorns
70g fresh coconut, cut into small
   chunks (*see note on p.13*)
1 tsp sea salt
2 garlic cloves
Juice of 1 lime
1 small onion, chopped
1 small green mango,
   peeled and chopped (optional)
   (*see note on p.14*)

SERVES:
2 AS A
SNACK
PREP:
25 MINS,
PLUS
20 MINS
MARINATING
COOK:
10 MINS

· To make the spice paste, place a small, dry frying pan over a high heat and toast the cumin, chillies, curry leaves and peppercorns for 30 seconds until aromatic. Tip into a blender.

· Turn the heat down to medium-high and place the coconut chunks in the pan. Let them lightly brown all over for 2–3 minutes, turning frequently. Add to the blender along with the salt, garlic, lime juice, onion, mango (if using) and a splash of water. Whiz until you have a coarse paste; you can add more water if the paste needs to be loosened up. Place in a jar and keep in the fridge for up to 2–3 days.

- Season the fish well with salt and black pepper on both sides.

- Mix 3 tablespoons of the spice paste with the tomato purée in a bowl, spread this over the fish pieces and cover with cling film. Leave to marinate in the fridge for 20 minutes.

- Place a non-stick frying pan on a medium-high heat and cover the bottom of the pan liberally with vegetable oil. Fry the fish steaks in the oil for 2–3 minutes (be careful as hot oil may splutter).

- Check the underside of the fish. It should be a golden brown colour and this is when it's ready to be flipped over. Continue to cook for another 2–3 minutes on the other side. You want a nice, even, crispy coating all over and for the fish to be cooked throughout.

- Drain the fish on a plate lined with kitchen paper, then cut into smaller pieces, drizzle over some lemon or lime juice from the wedges and serve hot as a snack or alongside some rice.

The Seychelles are dotted with tropical breadfruit trees and there is a saying that if you eat breadfruit on the island you will always come back, so strong is its lure.

This green, cannonball-sized fruit has hard, creamy flesh mottled with tiny seeds. It can be mashed, boiled, baked in desserts or fried as a snack. Its name comes from the texture it has when cooked, which is similar to bread but with a potato-like flavour.

I met an elderly man at Beau Vallon market in the north, frying thinly sliced breadfruit and plantain, dropping them into a huge round-bottomed pan filled to the brim with hot oil. Seconds later they were cooked, scattered with sea salt and portioned off into bags to be sold. They were salty, addictively crunchy and all the more delicious for being freshly cooked. I devoured them with an ice-cold SeyBrew (the Seychelles' local beer) and went back for more.

BREADFRUIT CHIPS WITH PAPRIKA & SEA SALT
SEYCHELLES

600g breadfruit (approx. ½ fruit)
1 tsp sea salt, plus extra to season

1 litre vegetable oil, for deep frying
1 tsp paprika

SERVES:
4 AS A
SNACK
PREP:
20 MINS
COOK:
10 MINS

- Trim the breadfruit, peel the hard green skin, cut into quarters and remove the centre core so you are left with the white flesh. Further slice the breadfruit into thin slices using a mandolin (be careful of those fingers!) or with a sharp knife. Place them in a bowl, cover them with cold water and mix in the salt.

- Heat the oil in a deep, heavy-based pan, or in a deep fat fryer if you have one, to 210°C. Pat dry the breadfruit slices with kitchen paper to remove excess water. Fry in batches in the hot oil, gently moving them around the pan until they are light golden brown and crispy. This will take 1 minute for each batch.

- Using a slotted spoon, drain the chips and put on a large plate lined with kitchen paper to soak up the excess oil. Season with sea salt and sprinkle over a light dusting of paprika. Repeat with the remaining breadfruit slices and serve.

These crunchy, spicy lentil balls, similar to falafel or Indian 'vada', are one of the most popular street food snacks, or 'gajacks', in Mauritius. Yellow split peas are soaked in water overnight so they plump up and are easier to crush. They are then spiked with plenty of green chillies and fresh coriander before being rolled into small balls and deep fried. Eat them straight away, alongside other snacks like samosas (p.146) and dunked into Coriander green chilli chutney (p.190) or, like the locals do, stuffed into crusty baguettes.

CHILLI DHAL FRITTERS
GATEAUX PIMENTS, MAURITIUS

200g yellow split peas
3 spring onions, finely chopped
2 tbsp finely chopped coriander
2–3 green chillies, finely chopped

1 tsp salt
Freshly ground black pepper
1 litre vegetable oil, for deep frying

MAKES:
25 BALLS
PREP:
15 MINS,
PLUS
OVERNIGHT
SOAKING
COOK:
UNDER
5 MINS
PER BATCH

· Place the yellow split peas in a large bowl and cover with cold water. Leave to sit overnight and soak.

· The peas should have puffed up slightly and the water reduced by the next morning. Drain them well and tip into a food processor. Blitz until the peas are a coarse paste and clump together. Tip the crushed peas into a large mixing bowl and add all the other ingredients apart from the oil. Combine well with a spoon.

· Take a tablespoon of the mixture in your hands and, pressing firmly, form into a ball shape (about the size of a golf ball). Each will weigh around 25g and you should get 25 balls. Repeat with the remaining mixture and place them all on a plate ready to be fried.

· Pour the vegetable oil into a deep, heavy-based saucepan or deep fat fryer and heat to 180°C. You can tell when the oil is the right temperature by dropping a small cube of bread into the oil. If it browns evenly in 30 seconds then it is ready. When the oil is hot enough, carefully drop in the balls (about four or five at a time, to prevent overcrowding in the pan).

· The fritters should sizzle in the oil. Using a fork or a slotted spoon gently move them around so they colour evenly. It will take a couple of minutes until they are golden brown and cooked throughout. If they brown too quickly, reduce the heat slightly to make sure they cook inside.

· Drain on a wire rack with kitchen paper underneath to catch any excess oil. Serve with Coriander green chilli chutney or crushed into a crusty white baguette.

When you mention 'dhal puri' to any local from Mauritius, the response is usually a sigh of utter joy. These paper-thin flatbreads are filled with a crushed dhal mixture and seasoned with aromatic roasted cumin. They are almost always sold in pairs and street vendors work frantically to keep up with demand, quickly smearing a little butterbean 'cari', chilli paste or tomato chutney in the centre of each flatbread, then folding them over and serving like a wrap. You can easily devour two or three in a go. They would also be delicious with the Seychellois aubergine & chickpea cari (p.119) with some Green bean, cabbage & carrot mustard pickle (p.186) or a chilli sauce scattered over the top.

There are some tricks for making thin, light 'dhal puri'. It's important to leave the dough to rest and soften, and to crush the paste so there are no hard bits remaining that may puncture the dough. Try to roll the 'puri' as thin as you can and keep a close eye on them in the pan as they only take a few seconds to cook. To keep them soft, take them off the heat before any brown spots start appearing.

CUMIN & LENTIL FLATBREADS
DHAL PURI, MAURITIUS

Vegetable oil, for frying

For the filling:
100g yellow split peas
1 tsp ground turmeric
1 tsp sea salt
1 tsp cumin seeds or ground cumin

For the dough:
250g plain flour,
  plus extra for kneading
½ tsp baking powder
Pinch of sea salt
1 tbsp vegetable oil,
  plus extra for oiling

MAKES:
12 SMALL
FLATBREADS

PREP:
50 MINS,
PLUS
OVERNIGHT
SOAKING

COOK:
35 MINS
FOR LENTILS,
AROUND
1 MIN
FOR EACH
FLATBREAD

· Place the yellow split peas in a large mixing bowl filled with cold water and leave to soak overnight.

· The following day, drain the yellow split peas and place into a large, deep saucepan. Add 1 litre water and bring to the boil. Once it is boiling, add the turmeric and salt and bring down to a medium heat. Let this cook uncovered for 25–35 minutes, until the peas are just cooked – if you press one between your fingers it should crush easily.

· Once cooked, drain the peas and keep the cooking liquid in a separate bowl. The liquid will be used to make the dough later as it has extra flavour, so it's not to be wasted! Set the peas aside to cool down completely.

- Meanwhile, in a small, dry frying pan, toast the cumin seeds (or ground cumin) for 30 seconds until fragrant and grind to a powder using a pestle and mortar. Set aside.

- In a large mixing bowl, put the flour, baking powder, salt and oil and gradually add 150ml of the reserved cooking liquid (it's fine if it's still warm) to create a ball of dough. If it's too dry add a little more water, and if it's too wet add some flour until it's the right consistency.

- Knead this for 5 minutes on a lightly floured work surface until the dough is soft and smooth. When poked lightly with your finger it should slowly spring back. Form into a ball, then smear the dough all over with a little oil and place in a bowl. Cover with cling film and leave to rest for 30 minutes.

- In a food processor, blitz the cooked split peas until you have a smooth yellow powder that clumps together. Add in the ground cumin and mix together well.

- Flour a work surface and a rolling pin. Divide the dough into 12 balls, about 3cm in size. Take one piece and flatten into a circle using your fingers, cup the piece in your palm and fill with 2–3 teaspoons of filling. Pinch the edges to enclose the filling securely back into the shape of a ball. Repeat with remaining pieces.

- Roll the balls into circles about 3mm thin, turning 90 degrees every now and then. Make sure the surface is floured well to prevent the dough sticking or splitting.

- Brush a *tawa* (flat cast-iron pan) or non-stick pan with a smear of oil and place on a medium-high heat. Add one flatbread and cook for 30 seconds, then brush liberally with oil, flip over and cook for another 30 seconds. (If dark brown spots appear, it is cooking too quickly so reduce the heat slightly.) Sometimes they will also puff up, which is a good sign!

- Once cooked, the flatbreads will be a light yellow colour. Place them on a plate lined with kitchen paper, and repeat the process with the rest of the flatbreads, putting a sheet of greaseproof paper in between to stop them steaming or sticking together.

- These are best eaten straight away. Traditionally they are filled with chutney and a little curry, but you can also enjoy them just as they are or smeared with some butter. The flatbreads can also be cooled, then wrapped in foil or placed in a Tupperware, and kept in the freezer. To reheat, warm them in the microwave for 1 minute on full power, or defrost them fully and then warm through in the oven.

Pictured overleaf

A version of this snack is sold by street vendors across Mauritius. Chilli peppers are stuffed with a variety of fillings – tuna with cheese, chilli minced meat or mashed sardines – before being dipped in a chickpea-flour batter and deep fried.

Here I've used small baby peppers, which you can easily find in the supermarket, or if you come across long Turkish-style peppers, they will work well too. The mashed sardines, chilli and onion are spooned into the sweet peppers and baked in the oven rather than deep fried, making a mouthwatering snack or starter. For a vegetarian version, stuff them with cheese (such as mozzarella), fresh sweetcorn and finely chopped shallots.

STUFFED PEPPERS WITH SARDINES & CHILLI
PIMENT FARCI, MAURITIUS

200g sweet baby peppers
120g tin sardines in oil, drained
1 small red onion, finely chopped
1 red chilli, finely chopped
1 tbsp finely chopped coriander

Juice of ¼ lemon
Olive oil, for drizzling
Sea salt and freshly ground
    black pepper

SERVES:
4–6
PREP:
15 MINS
COOK:
30 MINS

· Preheat the oven to 200°C/Fan 180°C/Gas 6. Slice the peppers in half lengthways, while trying to keep the stalks on. Gently scoop out the seeds with a teaspoon and discard.

· Place the drained sardines in a medium-sized mixing bowl. Mash with a fork until there are no clumps, then add in the onion, chilli, coriander and lemon juice with some salt and pepper and mix well. Taste for seasoning.

· Next, spoon the mixture into the pepper halves.

· Place all the peppers on a lined baking tray and drizzle with olive oil. Put on the top shelf of the oven and cook for around 30 minutes until the peppers have softened and are tender when pierced with a fork. Serve immediately.

Juicy brochettes of marinated beef, sizzling on the barbecue or grill, are a regular sight in Madagascar. Pieces of 'zebu' – a type of humped cow – are marinated in soy sauce, ginger, garlic, honey and papaya, resulting in flavourful, juicy and tender meat. I have added a West African-style peanut–coconut sauce for dipping (I am a peanut addict). Serve the brochettes with the sauce as a snack, or with boiled manioc (cassava) or piled onto rice for something more substantial.

GRILLED BEEF SKEWERS WITH PEANUT SAUCE
MASIKITA, MADAGASCAR

500g beef (frying steak or rib-eye),
   cut into 3cm pieces
Olive oil, for drizzling
1 courgette, cut into small chunks
1 green pepper, cut into 3cm pieces
Lime wedges, to serve

For the marinade:
2 tbsp light soy sauce
2.5cm piece of fresh root ginger,
   peeled and grated
2 garlic cloves, finely chopped
1 tbsp honey
40g green papaya, grated
   (or you can use juice of ½ lemon)
1 tbsp olive oil
Freshly ground black pepper

For the peanut dipping sauce:
1 tbsp olive oil
1 shallot, finely chopped
1 garlic clove, finely chopped
1 tsp ground ginger
2 tbsp good-quality
   smooth peanut butter
1 tbsp light soy sauce
1 tbsp dark brown sugar
200ml coconut milk
Juice of ½ lime

6 wooden skewers, soaked in water
   for 30 minutes

MAKES:
6 SKEWERS
PREP:
35 MINS,
PLUS
AT LEAST
2 HOURS
MARINATING
COOK:
15 MINS

· Firstly put all the marinade ingredients and the beef in a large freezer bag or bowl, and combine well until all the meat is covered. Leave to marinate in the fridge overnight (or for at least 2 hours).

· Next, make the peanut sauce. Heat the olive oil in a shallow frying pan over a medium heat, then add the shallot, garlic and ginger. Cook for 5 minutes, stirring occasionally, until the shallot has softened. Stir in the peanut butter, soy sauce and brown sugar and cook for a minute or two.

- Pour in the coconut milk, whisk together well and simmer for a further 5 minutes. The sauce will thicken and reduce slightly. Check for seasoning and squeeze over the lime juice. Place the sauce in a small bowl, keeping 2 tablespoons aside for basting the skewers.

- Preheat a grill to medium-high. Drizzle some olive oil over the courgette and pepper. Using the wooden skewers, start threading through alternately the marinated meat, pepper and courgette until all the meat and vegetables have been used up.

- Place the skewers on a wire rack under the grill for around 10 minutes in total, turning over three times during the cooking time and basting with the peanut sauce that was kept aside. Grill until the beef is cooked to how you like it and the vegetables are slightly softened and charred.

- Serve the brochettes with the peanut dipping sauce and lime wedges.

COMOROS
AND
MAYOTTE

TAKING THEIR NAME from the Arabic word *qamar* meaning 'moon', the islands that make up the Comoro archipelago – together they are Comoros and Mayotte – are quite different to those in the rest of this book. They're very definitely African and also mostly Muslim. Locals call their country Masiwa, which is simply translated as 'the islands'. The Union of the Comoros consists of Ngazidja (Grande Comore), Nzwani and Mwali. Mayotte voted to become a department of France in 2011 and it is far richer than its impoverished neighbours.

Sometimes known as the Perfume Islands, the scent of ylang-ylang and cloves are heady in the air. Rich volcanic soil and a decent amount of rain means that vanilla grows particularly well here and scents what could be considered the islands' national dish – *langouste à la vanille* (lobster in vanilla sauce).

Colonised by Africans in the eighth century, Islam became the religion in the eleventh century, and is now practised by ninety-eight per cent of the population. Lying in the Indian Ocean between East Africa and Madagascar, the Comoros were first put on a European map by Portuguese cartographer Diego Ribero in 1527, and they soon became an important trading post for Persian, African and European traders. The Portuguese introduced products from the New World to the islands and many dishes include bell peppers, maize, chillies, tomatoes, bananas, pineapples, limes and oranges. Breadfruit, cassava (manioc), coconuts, bananas, sweet potatoes and plantains thrive here, but the staple of the diet – rice – has to be imported. The food here took a French twist when the islands were colonised in 1886.

You will also find South-Indian-style curries, African root vegetable stews and porridges, and particularly in Mayotte it is common to see Arab–French-inspired dishes. *Mkatra foutra* is a fried bread a bit like a pancake, made with coconut milk or water, sprinkled with sesame seeds and drizzled with honey – it is often eaten for breakfast with strong Arabic coffee.

Most weekends, families have a barbecue on the beach, called a *voulé*, where they make fires topped with metal grills on which they pile *mbawa* (chicken wings), *brochettes* (skewers of meat), goat and breadfruit – these are eaten with *pili pili*, a hot red sauce made from chilli peppers, cloves, garlic and lemon. Desserts are Indian-influenced with *ladu*, ground rice mixed with sugar and ghee and shaped into bricks, or *donas*, doughnuts made with sweetened condensed milk and vanilla then deep fried.

NGAZIDJA

Moroni

COMOROS

MWALI

NZWANI

Mamoudzou

MAYOTTE

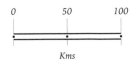

0   50   100

Kms

These flavourful patties, scented with cumin, coriander, hints of chilli spice and fresh mint, are what my mum calls 'Mauritian-style burgers'. She would make these when I was a child – they were slightly charred when cooked and oozed a little lamb juice when pressed between your fingers. You can either pop them straight in your mouth, dipped in some Sweet mango & red chilli chutney (p.194), chilli sauce or yoghurt, or sandwich them into a slider bun for the perfect burger. I love the sweetness of the cinnamon running through the patties – it goes so well with the lamb.

SPICY LAMB PATTIES
CATLESS, MAURITIUS

500g minced lamb
1 onion, finely chopped
2 garlic cloves, finely chopped
2–3 green chillies, seeds in, finely
   chopped, or 1 tsp chilli powder
2 tbsp chopped coriander
2 tbsp chopped mint
1 tsp ground cinnamon

1 tbsp light soy sauce
1 tsp ground cumin
1 tsp ground turmeric
1 egg, beaten
1 tbsp vegetable oil,
   plus extra for your hands
Sea salt and freshly ground
   black pepper

MAKES:
12 PATTIES
PREP:
15 MINS
COOK:
10 MINS

· In a medium-sized bowl, mix together all the ingredients except the oil, with some salt and pepper, using your hands to really work the mixture for a few minutes to ensure all the spices are evenly distributed.

· Wash your hands and smear a little oil on your palms, which will help to shape the patties. Take small portions of the mince mixture and roll into 12 golf-ball-sized patties.

· Heat the oil in a large, non-stick frying pan over a medium-high heat. Place about half of the patties in the pan without overcrowding it. Squash them down gently using the back of a fork until they are around 1.5cm thick, and cook for 3 minutes until you see a brown crust forming underneath, then flip them over on to the other side. Cook for 3–5 minutes until cooked throughout.

· Transfer to a plate lined with kitchen paper to remove excess oil and cover lightly with foil to keep them warm while frying the remaining patties. Serve with chilli sauce, chutney or yoghurt to dip or stuff a couple into Curry leaf bread rolls (p.137) or shop-bought bread rolls with some crunchy lettuce to make delectable burgers.

Variation

· The recipe is for snack-sized patties, but you can make six larger ones from this recipe and use them for burgers if you wish.

Introduced to Réunion by Chinese immigrants from the Canton region, the 'bouchon' is now one of the island's most popular snacks. These zesty little steamed parcels are filled with seasoned minced pork or chicken and served with a soy and ginger dipping sauce. The traditional way to cook these is to use a bamboo steamer, which you can find in most Asian stores and supermarkets. I find adding a round of greaseproof paper or torn cabbage leaves in the base of the steamer can stop the dumplings sticking.

Another version of these 'bouchons' is sold on food trucks as 'pain bouchon gratiné': a French baguette stuffed with the dumplings and liberally covered with melted cheese – to die for!

PORK DUMPLINGS WITH SOY GINGER DIP
BOUCHONS, RÉUNION

500g minced pork
2 spring onions, finely chopped
3 kaffir lime leaves, finely chopped,
    or zest of 1 lime
2 tbsp light soy sauce
1 tbsp grated fresh root ginger
1 tsp chilli flakes
Plain flour, for dusting
1 pack of chilled wonton
    pastry wrappers (available
    from Asian supermarkets)
Freshly ground black pepper

For the dipping sauce:
4 tbsp light soy sauce
2 tbsp sesame oil
2 tbsp rice wine vinegar
2 tsp brown sugar
1 red chilli, finely chopped
1 tbsp finely chopped chives

MAKES:
APPROX.
24 DUMPLINGS
PREP:
25 MINS
COOK:
10 MINS
PER BATCH

· First, make the dipping sauce. Mix all the ingredients together well in a small bowl and leave aside to infuse while you make the dumplings.

· In a large mixing bowl, add the minced pork, spring onion, kaffir lime leaves, soy sauce, ginger, chilli and pepper to season. Mix well.

· To assemble the dumplings, dust some flour on to a work surface and fill a small glass with some cold water. Take the first wonton pastry wrapper and place in a diamond shape with a corner, not an edge, nearest to you.

· Using your finger, slightly dampen all edges of the wrapper with the water; this will help it stick together. Take 1 scant tablespoon of the pork mixture, shape it into a ball and place in the centre of the wrapper.

- Take the corner closest to you and the opposite corner and bring those together, sealing the edge. Then bring up the other two corners into the centre, scrunching them into a little pouch. The pork filling should be well enclosed, but add a little more water to completely seal the edges if needed.

- Repeat with the remaining wonton pastry to make all your dumplings. A few extra hands help and make it fun! (Leftover wrappers will keep in a sealed container in the fridge for a week or so.)

- Put a few of the dumplings in a single layer inside a bamboo steamer lined with greaseproof paper or torn cabbage leaves, leaving some space between them so they don't stick together. Put the steamer over a pan of simmering water, cover and cook for around 10 minutes until the pork is cooked throughout. When they're done, the wrappers will appear translucent and the filling opaque. You can cut one open to check. Take them out gently with tongs, then steam the rest of the dumplings in batches. Serve immediately, bundled onto a platter with the dipping sauce.

A 'sundowner' is the Mauritian tradition of having a snack with a chilled beer or cocktail at sunset, and these fritters go perfectly with my Lychee, rum & lime ti punch (p.241). That initial sizzle of battered prawns in the pan makes my stomach rumble as I anticipate sinking my teeth through the golden crust into the perfectly succulent prawn inside.

These fritters should be eaten straight away while they are still crisp, and are delicious dunked into chilli sauce or Coriander green chilli chutney (p.190).

CHILLI PRAWN FRITTERS
CREVETTES CROUSTILLANTES, MAURITIUS

150g fresh raw king prawns, peeled, deveined and cleaned
1 tbsp finely chopped spring onion
1 green chilli, finely sliced
1 lemon, ½ juiced and the rest cut into wedges
2.5cm piece of fresh root ginger, peeled and finely chopped
1 garlic clove, finely chopped
1 tsp light soy sauce
500ml vegetable oil, for deep frying

1 small bunch of coriander, leaves picked and chopped
Sea salt and freshly ground black pepper

For the batter:
30g cornflour
30g plain flour
30ml chilled water
1 egg, beaten

SERVES:
2
PREP:
15 MINS, PLUS 15 MINS MARINATING
COOK:
5 MINS

- Place the prawns, spring onion, chilli, lemon juice, ginger, garlic and soy sauce in a mixing bowl, mix together well with a spoon, add a sprinkling of black pepper and salt, then set aside to marinate for 15 minutes.

- Pour the vegetable oil into a deep, heavy-based pan, or use a deep fat fryer if you have one, and heat to 180°C or until a small piece of bread turns golden brown within 30 seconds of dropping it into the oil.

- Meanwhile, in another medium-sized mixing bowl, combine the flours, then add in the water and beaten egg. Use a whisk to gently incorporate all the ingredients into a batter; it doesn't matter too much if there are a few lumps.

- Remove the prawns from the marinade and pat dry with kitchen paper. Once the oil is hot enough, dip the prawns one by one into the batter and lower them gently into the hot oil. Fry for 2 minutes or so until lightly browned and crisp.

- Drain the prawns on a wire rack with kitchen paper underneath to catch any excess oil and serve immediately with the coriander scattered on top and the lemon wedges and a chutney or chilli sauce on the side.

These palm-sized soft flatbreads are made with smoked tuna and a coconut dough in the Maldives. The tuna is caught daily and dried in the sun, fresh coconut is scraped or grated and the curry leaves are plucked straight off the trees. These moreish snacks have just the right balance of chilli heat, refreshing coconut sweetness and that irresistible flavour of the sea that is synonymous with island life.

Desiccated, unsweetened coconut can be used instead of grated coconut – soak it first in warm water to rehydrate. If you have any leftover tuna and coconut mixture, it is also traditionally eaten for breakfast ('mas huni') with plain 'roshi' (Maldivian flatbreads) or I find it works wonderfully over fresh salad leaves and drizzled with olive oil to serve.

TUNA & COCONUT FLATBREADS
MASROSHI, MALDIVES

For the filling:
10 curry leaves, fresh or dried, finely
    chopped, or 1 tbsp curry powder
2.5cm piece of fresh root ginger,
    peeled and finely grated
2 garlic cloves, finely chopped
1 small onion, finely chopped
1 chilli ('Githeyo mirus'/'Scotch bonnet'
    or 'Habanero'), finely chopped
Zest and juice of ½ lemon
1 tsp sea salt
160g tin tuna in water, well drained
100g freshly grated coconut (*see note
    on p.13*), excess water squeezed out
    with your hands

For the dough:
500g plain flour, sifted,
    plus extra for rolling
2 tsp sea salt
100ml vegetable oil
170ml warm water

MAKES:
12 FLATBREADS
PREP:
1½ HOURS
COOK:
15 MINS
PER BATCH
(3 BATCHES,
AROUND
45 MINS)

- Place the curry leaves, ginger, garlic, onion, chilli, lemon zest, juice and salt in a large mixing bowl and combine well. Incorporate the tuna and grated coconut into the mixture, using the back of a fork to press the mixture together so it creates a paste-like texture.

- In another large bowl, add the sifted flour and salt and mix together. Create a well in the middle of the bowl and pour in the oil. Use your fingertips to mix the oil with the flour until a light breadcrumb texture is achieved. Slowly add in the warm water a little at a time while mixing to create a dough. Add a little more flour or water until it's soft and pliable, not sticky or too dry. Use your hands to knead the dough on a lightly floured work surface for 1–2 minutes until soft and smooth.

· Divide the dough into 12 round balls of similar size. Take one dough ball and press it into the palm of your hand to make a cupped shape. Take 2 teaspoons of the tuna mixture and put it into the centre of the dough. Press the edges of the dough together to enclose the mixture inside. Pinch the top to ensure nothing comes out. Repeat with the rest of the mixture and dough balls.

· Once they are all filled, take one and lay it on a lightly floured surface. Using a rolling pin, gently roll the dough ball into a circular shape about 8cm in diameter. Repeat with the rest and set aside.

· Preheat the oven to 190°C/Fan 170°C/Gas 5 and place a large non-stick frying pan or *tawa* (similar to a crêpe pan) over a medium heat on the hob. Take your flatbreads and place them on the dry pan; you can probably fit three or four at a time. Cook for 3 minutes, then flip to the other side for 3 minutes until they have golden-brown specks on both sides. Place in the oven for 10 minutes until puffed up slightly and cooked throughout. Repeat with the rest and serve on a plate. They are best eaten straight away while they're still warm.

Variation

· To replicate the subtle smoky flavour of the *masroshi* made in the Maldives, add 1 teaspoon of smoked paprika to the mixture.

Pictured overleaf

My parents often reminisce about growing up in Mauritius, when fresh fish was so expensive that using tinned alternatives to tuna or sardines was a necessity. My dad still likes to mash tinned sardines with raw onions, chillies and a little tomato and serve it in a French baguette, but my favourite use for them is making bite-size croquettes for an afternoon snack.

The rich flavour of sardines mellows when cooked, and here it is uplifted with lemon zest and hints of chilli. It makes for an irresistible croquette when mixed with creamy mashed potatoes and covered in a golden brown breadcrumb coating. Serve on a platter with chilli sauce or Green chilli paste with lemon (p.197) and lemon wedges.

SARDINE CROQUETTES
BOULETTES SARDINE, MAURITIUS

3 medium potatoes (500g),
  peeled and cut into quarters
1 medium courgette (200g),
  coarsely grated
1 medium carrot (140g)
3 thyme sprigs, leaves picked
20g coriander, leaves picked
  and finely chopped
2 green chillies, seeds in, finely
  chopped

120g tin sardines in oil,
  drained and mashed well
1 lemon, zest grated
  and then cut into wedges
4 tbsp plain flour
2 eggs, beaten
100g panko breadcrumbs
1 litre vegetable oil, for deep frying
Sea salt and freshly ground
  black pepper

MAKES:
20 CROQUETTES
PREP:
40 MINS
COOK:
5 MINS

· Bring a large saucepan of water to the boil with ½ teaspoon salt and add in the potatoes. Cook for 20 minutes until just tender, with a slight bite.

· While the potatoes are boiling, place the grated courgette in a medium-sized mixing bowl, add ½ teaspoon salt, mix well, and leave it to sit for 15 minutes – this will draw out the excess water. After 15 minutes, use your hands to squeeze out the water over the sink.

- Next, grate the carrot into the same bowl as the courgette and add the thyme, coriander, chilli, sardines and lemon zest. Mix this well until all the ingredients are combined.

- Once the potatoes are cooked, drain them in a colander and mash with a potato masher until completely smooth. Add the potatoes to the sardine mixture and, using the back of a fork, mash everything together well. Season with salt and pepper.

- Take a golf-ball-sized amount of the mixture in your hands and, using your palms, roll into a ball. Place on a plate and repeat with the remaining mixture (you should end up with about 20 croquettes). Cool them in the fridge for 15 minutes to firm up slightly.

- Set up one small plate with the plain flour, one small bowl with the beaten eggs and another bowl with breadcrumbs.

- Heat the oil in a deep, heavy-based pan or deep fat fryer to around 180°C (or when a piece of bread sizzles and turns golden in around 30 seconds). Take each croquette, dust in the flour, dip into the egg and then roll in the breadcrumbs, ensuring an even coating. You don't want to overcrowd the pan, so you will need to fry the croquettes in batches. Lower a few croquettes gently into the hot oil with a slotted spoon and, using a fork, turn them occasionally to get an even golden brown colour all over. Each batch should take around 1–2 minutes.

- Drain the croquettes on a wire rack with kitchen paper underneath to catch the excess oil. Serve immediately with chilli sauce or chilli paste and the lemon wedges.

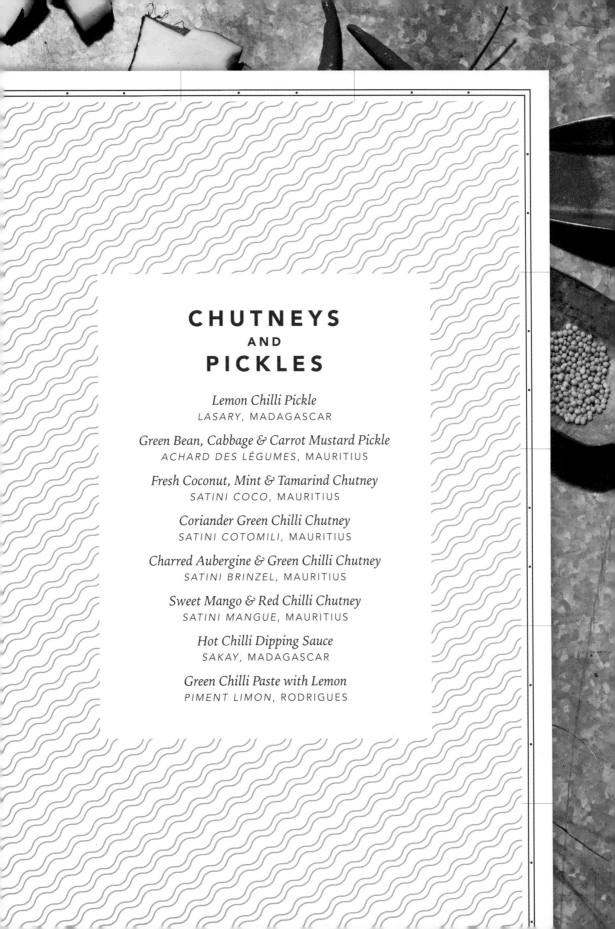

CHUTNEYS
AND
PICKLES

Lemon Chilli Pickle
LASARY, MADAGASCAR

Green Bean, Cabbage & Carrot Mustard Pickle
ACHARD DES LÉGUMES, MAURITIUS

Fresh Coconut, Mint & Tamarind Chutney
SATINI COCO, MAURITIUS

Coriander Green Chilli Chutney
SATINI COTOMILI, MAURITIUS

Charred Aubergine & Green Chilli Chutney
SATINI BRINZEL, MAURITIUS

Sweet Mango & Red Chilli Chutney
SATINI MANGUE, MAURITIUS

Hot Chilli Dipping Sauce
SAKAY, MADAGASCAR

Green Chilli Paste with Lemon
PIMENT LIMON, RODRIGUES

CHUTNEYS
AND
PICKLES

THE ZING AND spice of a pickle, chutney or condiment is an essential part of every meal on the Indian Ocean islands. With such an abundance of exotic fruit and vegetables grown in the tropical climate, it's not hard to see why. The process of macerating and preserving fresh produce to prolong its shelf life has been a tradition here for centuries, and making ingredients last as long as possible was a necessity – especially over the winter months. My nan would pickle jars of fruits, vegetables and chillies in oil and vinegar. They would then sit in the sun to cure for a few hours or even a whole day before being stacked in the cupboard or fridge, ready to emanate their exquisite aromas when opened.

However, in Mauritius it's not uncommon to buy your pickles from the *marchands confits*, or pickle sellers, who hawk their wares from wheeled carts or stalls laden with enormous jars of pickled fruits and vegetables. They use green mangoes, sliced pineapple, giant green olives, chou chou and fruit de cythère (also known as June plums) to make their pickles. These mouthwatering sour treats are something I always look forward to, stopping at the roadside to buy a small cellophane bag of whatever pickle takes my fancy and enjoying it doused in tamarind, chilli flakes and salt, with extra bags to take home for the family.

My favourite pickles are those using diced green mango, chunks of pineapple, golden apple or lemon, such as the Lemon chilli pickle from Madagascar (p.185). The addition of chillies, ginger, garlic and vinegar creates the perfect medley of sour and spice, infusing the natural juices over time. A quicker, more instant way of making pickles is to grate, slice or chop vegetables and stir-fry them in a mix of heady spices, usually garlic, chilli, turmeric and mustard seeds – try the Green bean, cabbage & carrot mustard pickle on p.186. This is usually eaten either straight away or the next day after the flavours have had time to mingle, although it will last for a few days in the fridge.

The chutneys in this chapter are very different from the jam-like confections you find on supermarket shelves in the West. Chutneys are made as needed, using fresh ingredients that are blended or mixed together just before serving. Recipes like the Coriander green chilli chutney (p.190) are simple to make and are an essential accompaniment to snacks and street food (pp.140–179). Fresh coconut makes a sprightly chutney when combined with mint and tamarind (p.189), while the Sweet mango & red chilli chutney (p.194) is delicious with fish and seafood.

This pickled lemon condiment, with its zesty segments and fiery chilli finish, is a speciality of Réunion and Madagascar. The 'lasary' uses 'Piri piri', a chilli pepper from Africa that can be sourced online either dried or ground in a powder, but if you can't find it, the bird's eye or finger chillies found in supermarkets will do.

The slow macerating time is well worth the wait: the spicy and sour work in beautiful harmony. A spoonful of this pickle goes well alongside the robust Fragrant goat cooked in masala spices (p.48) and grilled or barbecued fish like Sardines with lemon, chilli & paprika (p.90). You can also use it as a salad dressing mixed with a little olive oil, salt and pepper.

LEMON CHILLI PICKLE
LASARY, MADAGASCAR

8 large lemons (1kg)
2 tsp sea salt
1 onion, thinly sliced
4 red chillies, thinly sliced
200ml lemon juice (approx. 7 lemons)

250ml white wine vinegar
2cm piece of fresh root ginger, peeled and grated
2 garlic cloves, grated
1 tbsp mild curry powder

MAKES:
4 X 250ML JARS
PREP:
30 MINS, PLUS
24 HOURS MACERATING, PLUS
1 WEEK FERMENTING

· Wash and pat the lemons dry and grate the lemon zest into a large bowl, taking as little of the bitter pith as possible. Slice the base and top off the lemons so they sit flat on the chopping board. Use a sharp knife or vegetable peeler to remove the remaining peel and white pith from the lemons, then discard. Holding the fruit over the bowl to catch any juice, cut along either side of the white membrane to remove the segments. Place the segments in the bowl with the zest.

· Add the salt and sliced onion to the bowl. Mix well, cover with cling film and leave at room temperature for 24 hours, stirring occasionally.

· After the lemons have macerated in the salt, add the chilli, lemon juice, vinegar, ginger, garlic and curry powder. Stir to combine. Store in sterilised jars (see note below) and keep them in the fridge.

· Leave to ferment for at least 7 days in the fridge. The pickle is best eaten within a month.

How to sterilise jars

· Preheat the oven to 140°C/Fan 120°C/Gas 1. Wash the jars and lids in hot soapy water, then rinse well. Place on a baking tray and pop into the oven for 10–15 minutes until dry throughout. They are now ready to use.

The traditional preparation of achard pickle always involves the grinding of black mustard and fenugreek seeds on the 'roche cari' (grinding stone). I would watch my Nani (Dad's mum) do this in the back garden of the family home in Mauritius. She would slowly add chilli, garlic, fresh turmeric and a little water, crushing it against the stone with a large rolling pin until a vivid yellow paste formed. Blanched vegetables were then turned in the aromatic paste, decanted into jars and left to marinate in the fridge before eating.

The pickle is delicious sandwiched into a baguette with some Chilli dhal fritters (p.156) or is a great accompaniment to a 'cari' or Fish biryani (p.92).

GREEN BEAN, CABBAGE & CARROT MUSTARD PICKLE
ACHARD DES LÉGUMES, MAURITIUS

200g carrots, peeled and sliced into batons (5mm thick and 7cm long)
200g white cabbage, finely sliced
200g green beans, trimmed and sliced
½ tsp fenugreek seeds (or use ground)
1 tsp ground turmeric
2 tsp black mustard seeds
3 tbsp vegetable oil

1 garlic clove, finely chopped
1–2 red chillies, sliced
¼ small onion, finely sliced
2 tbsp white wine vinegar
1 tsp sea salt

Ice cubes

MAKES:
750G
PICKLE
PREP:
20 MINS
COOK:
UNDER
5 MINS

· Fill a large bowl with cold water and ice cubes and set aside (this will be used for dunking your blanched vegetables).

· Place a large pan of boiling water on a high heat, tip all your prepared carrots, cabbage and green beans into the water and, using a slotted spoon, ensure they are submerged. Bring back to the boil, let the vegetables boil away for 1 minute, then drain them and tip into the ice-cold water for 1 minute to arrest the cooking process. This helps them retain a nice crunchy texture.

· Drain the vegetables, spread them out on a baking tray and pat dry with kitchen paper.

· Next make the spice paste. Using a pestle and mortar, grind together the fenugreek, turmeric and black mustard seeds and add a splash of water to make a coarse, wet paste.

- In a large frying pan over a medium heat, add the vegetable oil, and tip in the garlic, chilli and onion – they should start to gently sizzle and pop. Spoon in the spice paste and mix well in the oil for 30 seconds. Add in the blanched vegetables and mix until they have all turned a glorious yellow colour. Scatter over the vinegar (add more if desired) and salt and combine. Check for seasoning and spoon into jars. You can eat the pickle straight away or it will last well in the fridge for up to 1 week.

Variation

- The same spice mix can be used to make apple and carrot pickle (my mum makes this at home). Dice 2 carrots and 1 'tart' apple (cooking apples work well) and mix together in a bowl. Add in 2 finely chopped deseeded green chillies, combine with the spice paste cooked by the same method above, and finally add salt to taste. Store in jars or an airtight container in the fridge for up to 1 week.

Here, toasted coconut, fresh mint leaves and tangy tamarind make a smooth chutney that will transport you to the coastal shores of Mauritius with its overhanging coconut palms. This chutney is a must when eating 'gajacks' (snacks) like Potato & pea samosas (p.146) and pairs perfectly with fish dishes or alongside a Traditional-style beef cari (p.44).

I toast the coconut in a pan to enhance its flavour and lend it that slightly toasted taste – it makes such a difference to the end result. If you don't have any tamarind, I find adding a squeeze of lemon or lime achieves a similar result.

FRESH COCONUT, MINT & TAMARIND CHUTNEY
SATINI COCO, MAURITIUS

1 tbsp vegetable oil
1 small coconut or 150g peeled white flesh, grated *(see note on p.13)*
1 tsp tamarind paste or pulp *(see note on p.20)*

Pinch of caster sugar
½ tsp flaky sea salt
2–3 red chillies, seeds in
1 small bunch of mint, leaves picked

MAKES:
AROUND
225G
CHUTNEY

PREP:
20 MINS

COOK:
UNDER
5 MINS

- In a large frying pan over a medium-high heat, pour in the vegetable oil, scatter in the grated coconut and toast the flesh for 2–3 minutes until you get a roasted coconut aroma and the flesh is slightly tinged brown but not burnt. This is to release the juices and flavour. Set aside to cool slightly.

- In a blender add the coconut, tamarind, sugar, salt, red chillies and mint leaves. Add 2 tablespoons water to get things going, then pulse in the blender, slowly adding more water until you have a slightly coarse paste. Check for seasoning and add more salt if needed. Store in a jar in the fridge and consume within 2–3 days.

There is no more versatile herb in the world than vibrant, aromatic coriander. One of the special ways we use this herb in Mauritius is blended with chillies, garlic, tomatoes and lemon in a vivid green dip called 'cotomili'. A large amount of coriander is used, but it will all be whizzed down and concentrated in taste (you can keep the leftover stems in the fridge and finely chop them into dishes – they carry lots of aroma).

The chutney is eaten as a dip with snacks like Potato & pea samosas (p.146) and Chilli dhal fritters (p.156), and it can be used as an excellent marinade for fresh fish before cooking on the barbecue, or you can serve it alongside most dishes as a condiment.

CORIANDER GREEN CHILLI CHUTNEY

SATINI COTOMILI, MAURITIUS

2 ripe tomatoes (220g),
  roughly chopped
60g or 2 bunches of coriander,
  leaves roughly chopped

1 garlic clove
2–3 green chillies
½ tsp sea salt
Squeeze of lemon juice

MAKES:
AROUND
300G
CHUTNEY
PREP:
5 MINS

· Place the tomatoes and coriander in a blender followed by the garlic clove, chillies, salt, lemon and 2 tablespoons water. Give it a good whiz for a couple of minutes until the ingredients are blended well into a smooth chutney. If it's too dry, add a splash more water.

· Check for seasoning and add more salt if needed. You can also add more chilli if you want more of a kick. Decant into jars or keep it covered and in the fridge until serving. It will last a few days at its best.

My dad is in charge of making this at home: he takes infinite care over preparing the aubergine, carefully mashing the cooked flesh with a fork. I find you can roast the aubergine in the oven for a soft, mashable centre or – like the Middle Eastern technique – it can be grilled whole while held with tongs directly over the fire (or gas hob) for a more intense, smoky flavour.

This is a great side for barbecued dishes as it adds a mellow, soft texture, with sprightly pops of chilli, or it makes a lovely dip for warm grilled breads. The fresh, grassy coriander leaves finish it off nicely.

CHARRED AUBERGINE & GREEN CHILLI CHUTNEY
SATINI BRINZEL, MAURITIUS

2 large aubergines
Olive oil
2 green chillies, finely chopped
1 small red onion, finely sliced
1 tsp salt

2 tsp white wine vinegar
1 garlic clove, finely chopped
2 tbsp finely chopped coriander
Freshly ground black pepper

SERVES:
4
PREP:
20 MINS
COOK:
1 HOUR

- Preheat the oven to 200°C/Fan 180°C/Gas 6. Rub the aubergines all over with olive oil, put them in a roasting tray, then roast in the oven for 1 hour, turning occasionally, until completely softened. For a smokier flavour in the chutney, place the whole aubergine on the barbecue until soft or cook it over an open flame on the hob, turning with tongs, until the skin has blackened.

- In the meantime, place the green chillies, red onion, salt, vinegar, garlic and 2 tablespoons olive oil in a pestle and mortar. Pound together so the garlic and chillies are crushed and everything is mixed well.

- Once the aubergine is cooked, leave to cool slightly. Scoop out all the soft pulp into a large mixing bowl and, using a fork, mash the aubergine until it's soft. Tip in the onion mixture and scatter over the coriander leaves, mixing well with a spoon. Check for seasoning and add more salt if needed and some black pepper. Store in the fridge for 1–2 days.

This refreshing Mauritian chutney combines juicy mangoes, spicy red chilli, pungent garlic and a splash of vinegar. It doesn't matter if the mango is slightly under-ripe – it will soften once cooked. The combination of sweet fruit and fiery chilli is something that's common on the island, enjoyed often in pickles, chutneys or just as fruit covered in chilli salt as a snack.

This is perfect alongside Ginger & herb grilled red snapper (p.81), as a dip for Chilli prawn fritters (p.173) or alongside a plate of Sticky chicken with garlic & ginger (p.27). It's also great paired with some mature cheese and a hunk of baguette.

SWEET MANGO & RED CHILLI CHUTNEY
SATINI MANGUE, MAURITIUS

4 mangoes (approx. 700g flesh)
2–3 red chillies,
   deseeded and chopped
100ml cider vinegar
100g caster sugar

2 garlic cloves, grated
2cm piece of fresh root ginger,
   peeled and grated
2 tsp nigella seeds

MAKES:
1 X 250ML
JAR
PREP:
10 MINS
COOK:
40 MINS

· Peel and de-stone the mangoes and roughly chop the flesh (see note on p.14).

· In a saucepan over a medium heat, add the mango flesh, chilli, vinegar, sugar, garlic, ginger and nigella seeds. Stir well to combine, reduce the heat to a low simmer and cook for 35 minutes until reduced to a thick and syrupy chutney. Stir occasionally while cooking to ensure the sugar doesn't stick to the bottom of the pan.

· Let the chutney cool slightly, store in a sterilised jar (see note on p.185) and keep in the fridge for up to 1 month.

This red hot chilli pepper condiment is found in almost every Malagasy kitchen. The island's cuisine is not particularly spicy, but a homemade chilli sauce of some kind is always offered on the side to add a little kick to the dishes on the family dinner table.

'Sakay' means 'spicy' and it certainly lives up to its name. It is made with tiny red 'Sakay' chillies harvested in Madagascar, but I have used similar Thai red chillies to recreate the flavour.

This is great served with Grilled beef skewers with peanut sauce (p.164) and Beef & pork stew with spring greens (p.43) and can be used as a spicy sauce alongside most snacks and main dishes.

HOT CHILLI DIPPING SAUCE
SAKAY, MADAGASCAR

10 Thai red chillies
2.5cm piece of fresh root ginger, peeled and sliced
1 garlic clove

½ tsp sea salt
1 tsp white vinegar
Vegetable oil (approx. 4 tbsp)

MAKES:
AROUND
85G SAUCE
PREP:
5 MINS

· Place the chillies, ginger, garlic, salt and vinegar in a blender and pulse together. Then, with the blender on, slowly incorporate the oil until a smooth paste is achieved.

· Use this sauce sparingly: a dab or a small teaspoon will probably suffice (it's very hot!).

· Store the sauce in a jar or airtight container and keep in the fridge for up to 2 weeks.

In Rodrigues, 'limon aigre doux' is a popular 'confit' (Creole for 'preserve'). The beautiful small lemons that grow on Rodrigues are placed whole in a jar and marinated in salt, then sliced and mixed with crushed chilli peppers, sugar and sometimes honey. The balance of tartness, sweetness and heat makes this exceptionally delicious. My version is uplifting and simple to make – in a matter of minutes you can have a jar in your fridge. You only need a small spoonful to appreciate the wonderful flavours.

When you deseed the chillies, make sure you wear gloves. If you would like it even spicier, keep the chilli seeds in. You can eat this as a dip with fried snacks like the Sardine croquettes (p.178) or alongside grilled or barbecued fish like the Ginger & herb grilled red snapper (p.81). It's a great condiment to have in the fridge for when you fancy something fresh and spicy.

GREEN CHILLI PASTE WITH LEMON
PIMENT LIMON, RODRIGUES

100g green chillies
1 garlic clove
Juice of 1 lemon
1 tbsp vegetable oil, or more if needed

1 tsp sea salt
1 tsp caster sugar
1 small bunch of mint,
   leaves picked

MAKES:
200G PASTE
PREP:
15 MINS

· Remove the stalks from the chillies, slice them lengthways and deseed them (use disposable gloves for this), or leave the seeds in if you wish.

· Place all the ingredients in a blender with 75ml water and blend well until you have a smooth paste. If you find your paste is not smooth enough, add 1 tablespoon of vegetable oil at a time and continue to blend. Check for seasoning and add more salt or sugar if needed.

· Store in a jar or airtight container in the fridge and use within 8–10 days.

DESSERTS

Banana Cake with Passion Fruit Sauce
GATEAU BANANE, SEYCHELLES

Tropical Fruit Salad with Vanilla Syrup
SALADY VOANKAZO, MADAGASCAR

Sweet Potato with Nutmeg & Cinnamon
LADOB, SEYCHELLES

Banana Fritters with Rosewater
DHONKEYO KAJURU, MALDIVES

Rum-soaked Raisin Bread Pudding
POUDINE, MADAGASCAR

Pineapple Upside-down Cake with Cardamom Cream
MAURITIUS

Mango & Lime Tarte Tatin
MAURITIUS

Rice Pudding with Vanilla, Cinnamon & Cardamom
KHEER, MAURITIUS

Coconut Ice Cream with Caramelised Pineapple
MAURITIUS

Sesame Coconut Flatbreads
MKATRA FOUTRA, COMOROS & MAYOTTE

Semolina Greo
HALWA, MAURITIUS

Cardamom Chocolate Mousse with Pistachios
RÉUNION

Papaya & Coconut Pie
TOURTE RODRIGUAISE, RODRIGUES

DESSERTS

THE EXOTIC FRUIT and spices that flourish in the tropical climates of the Indian Ocean islands – bananas, pineapples, mangoes, coconuts, papaya, cinnamon, cardamom, nutmeg and vanilla, not to mention the region's sugar cane rum – give a heady, aromatic warmth to their desserts. But not all the recipes in this chapter are fruit-based; the natural sweetness of vegetables like sweet potato, cassava and breadfruit make substantial puddings when cooked in coconut milk and sweet spices, such as the Sweet potato with nutmeg & cinnamon (p.207), while you'll also find grains such as rice and semolina used to make filling, warmth-inducing bowls of joy. I've included a recipe for Semolina greo (p.226), a dish that my mum still makes regularly at home. It's also always served as an offering at Hindu religious ceremonies, pilgrimages and prayers.

The recipes in this chapter cover a whole spectrum of desserts and sweets, from the indulgent Rum-soaked raisin bread pudding from Madagascar (p.210) to the lighter Tropical fruit salad with vanilla syrup (p.204), which simply allows the best, freshest fruits to shine in their natural ripeness and juices. And on a hot day, it's hard to resist my Coconut ice cream with caramelised pineapple (p.222). As a child some of my favourite sweet treats were deep fried: sweet potato and sugar-coconut cakes (*gateaux patate*), doughnuts soaked in rich syrups (*gulab jamun*) and buttery

Indian-inspired sweet *ladoos* were all guaranteed to bring a smile to my face. Banana fritters with rosewater (p.208) is one such delight.

The French–European influence on the islands is particularly apparent in the local patisseries and bakeries. Flaky sweet pastries, coconut tarts, croissants, cakes made with exotic fruits and the classic Mauritian treat *napolitaines* (pink iced shortbread biscuits) can be found on display behind glass cabinets, tempting passers-by in need of a sweet treat. Banana cake with passion fruit sauce (p.203) and Mango & lime tarte tatin (p.218) are two mouthwatering examples of European-inspired desserts that have been given their own island flavour.

With so many of the fruits and spices now readily available, you too will be able to create something utterly moreish to transport you to the spice gardens of these islands.

The best 'gateau banane' I've tasted was during a spontaneous pit stop whilst travelling through winding mountainous roads and crystal-blue coasts around Mahé, the largest island in Seychelles. It was in a tiny service shop selling all manner of bric-a-brac, and on the counter was a tempting display of homemade banana cake made with fruit from the trees in the owner's back garden. The sponge was unbelievably soft, moist and fluffy, and the passion fruit sauce drizzled over the top added a little exotic tang. A slice of this is perfect to graze on in the afternoon with a cup of tea or coffee.

BANANA CAKE WITH PASSION FRUIT SAUCE
GATEAU BANANE, SEYCHELLES

3 ripe bananas (250g peeled
   weight)
¼ tsp ground nutmeg
½ tsp vanilla extract
100g light soft brown sugar
140g unsalted butter, softened
2 eggs, beaten
140g self-raising flour, sifted

½ tsp baking powder
Pinch of salt
50ml whole milk

For the passion fruit sauce:
50g caster sugar
Pulp of 6 passion fruits

SERVES:
8
PREP:
20 MINS
COOK:
1 HOUR

· Preheat the oven to 170°C/Fan 150°C/Gas 4. Line a 2lb (900g) loaf tin with greaseproof paper.

· Slice 1 banana lengthways and set ½ aside. Mash the rest of the bananas in a bowl, add the nutmeg and vanilla and mix well. Set aside.

· Beat the sugar and butter together in a mixer or by hand for 10 minutes until creamy and pale in colour. Add in the eggs slowly while mixing, then sift in the flour, add the baking powder and salt and gently mix while adding the milk. Scoop in the mashed bananas and combine.

· Pour the cake mixture into the loaf tin, place the reserved banana half on top of the batter in the tin and bake in the oven for around 1 hour or until a skewer, when inserted, comes out clean.

· In the meantime, make the passion fruit sauce: place the sugar and passion fruit pulp in a saucepan over a medium-high heat. Simmer for 3–5 minutes until all the sugar has dissolved and the sauce has reduced slightly. Take off the heat and leave to cool. Pass the sauce through a strainer into a small bowl.

· When the cake has cooked, take out of the oven and leave in the tin for 10 minutes, then take out of the tin to cool a little on a wire rack.

· Lightly drizzle over the passion fruit sauce and serve warm, cut into slices.

The exotic flavours of lychee, pineapple, jackfruit and melon work in close harmony here, enhanced by a spiced vanilla syrup using the island's famous Madagascan bourbon vanilla pods.

It's fine to use tinned fruit if you can't get hold of fresh – in most supermarket sections you can source tinned (yellow) jackfruit and lychees in syrup or water. You can find plump Madagascan vanilla pods online, but these can be expensive so vanilla extract would be fine to use too.

TROPICAL FRUIT SALAD WITH VANILLA SYRUP

SALADY VOANKAZO, MADAGASCAR

200g pineapple flesh, cut into
   1cm cubes (*see note on p.14*)
½ cantaloupe melon (150g peeled),
   skin and seeds removed, cut into
   1cm cubes
200g drained tinned lychees,
   cut into halves (fresh if available,
   stones removed)
100g tinned jackfruit, cut into
   1cm pieces (optional)
150g strawberries, cut into quarters

For the vanilla syrup:
100g caster sugar
1 vanilla pod, split lengthways
   and seeds scraped out,
   or 1 tsp vanilla extract
Juice of ½ lime
Leaves of 1 mint sprig, chopped,
   to serve

SERVES:
6
PREP:
25 MINS,
PLUS
COOLING
COOK:
UNDER
5 MINS

- First make the vanilla syrup. In a saucepan over a medium heat, add 100ml water and the sugar and stir until the sugar has dissolved. Increase the heat and leave to simmer for 2 minutes to turn slightly syrupy. Remove from the heat and stir in the vanilla seeds, add in the pod and the lime juice. Leave to cool slightly.

- Mix all the fruit together in a large bowl.

- Pour the syrup over the fruit. Stir gently, transfer to serving bowls and scatter over the mint leaves to serve.

In Anse Royale, high in the hills of the Seychelles, I visited Le Jardin du Roi, a spice garden that is steeped in the island's history as a nineteenth-century spice trade hub. It is lush with the aromas of vanilla orchids, and you can just pluck the leaves off the cinnamon trees, slightly crushing them in your hand and inhaling that intense, warm fragrance. Overhanging evergreen trees are dotted with large, cream-coloured casings that protectively cocoon their small aromatic nutmeg pods.

This humble dessert is a celebration of those flavours. The idea of eating potatoes for pudding may be a surprising one, but it's very familiar in this part of the world; the combination of warm sweet potatoes, steeped in coconut milk and enrobed in strong spices marries so well. This dish can also be made with plantains, bananas or even breadfruit. Serve a small portion with chilled whipped cream or ice cream.

SWEET POTATO WITH NUTMEG & CINNAMON
LADOB, SEYCHELLES

2 medium sweet potatoes
  (400g), peeled
3 cinnamon sticks
1 vanilla pod, split lengthways
  and seeds scraped out

1 tbsp light soft brown sugar
¼ tsp ground nutmeg
Pinch of sea salt
400ml tin coconut milk

SERVES:
6
PREP:
15 MINS
COOK:
25 MINS

- Cut the potatoes lengthways, then in half again so you have 4 long pieces. Slice these in half lengthways (they don't all have to be the same size).

- Repeat with the rest of the sweet potato so you have 16 pieces in total. Place these in the base of a large, deep pan or flameproof casserole dish, so they all snugly fit together.

- Tuck the cinnamon sticks into any spaces between the potatoes, add the vanilla seeds, then lay the split pod on top. Scatter over the light brown sugar, nutmeg and salt. Finally pour over the coconut milk.

- Place the dish on a medium-high heat and bring up to a brisk boil. Let the potato cook for 10 minutes, uncovered. The liquid will reduce slightly. Turn down the heat to a low simmer, place a lid on the dish and cook for an additional 10 minutes or until the sweet potatoes are tender but not completely falling apart. The sauce will have reduced to a thick, glossy, light brown coating.

- Serve the *ladob* warm in bowls. I like mine topped with a little ice cream or whipped cream.

These fritters are made from ripe or over-ripe bananas mashed with sugar, flour, coconut and rosewater, which are then deep fried into dark brown, flavoursome bitefuls. I love the Persian twist with the floral elixir of rosewater that Maldivians frequently add to desserts (but do be careful when using it as only a hint is needed). Serve them warm as they are, or alongside some vanilla ice cream.

BANANA FRITTERS WITH ROSEWATER

DHONKEYO KAJURU, MALDIVES

2 large, ripe bananas (300g), mashed
50g caster sugar
1 tsp rosewater
40g freshly grated coconut (*see note on p.13*) or desiccated, unsweetened coconut

150g plain flour
1 tsp baking powder
1 litre vegetable oil, for deep frying
Icing sugar (optional)

MAKES:
15 FRITTERS
PREP:
20 MINS
COOK:
UNDER
5 MINS
PER BATCH

· In a large bowl, combine the mashed bananas with the sugar and mix well. Add in the rosewater and coconut and fold in the flour and baking powder.

· Heat the oil in a deep, heavy-based pan or deep fat fryer to 170°C. You can test this using a cooking thermometer or, alternatively, drop a 3cm cube of bread into the oil. If it takes around 60 seconds to brown, the oil is ready (take great care when doing this).

· Take a tablespoon of the mixture and gently drop it into the oil. Fry the banana fritters in batches to ensure thorough and even cooking – they will cook in around 2–3 minutes.

· Using a fork, gently flip over the fritters so they go a lovely golden brown all over. Remove with a slotted spoon, drain on kitchen paper, and serve immediately with some icing sugar dusted on top if you like.

Think of plump, boozy raisins clothed in a soft, sweet, warm bread pudding with a golden crust. The orange zest, floral vanilla, caramelised sugar and hint of rum make this dessert an indulgent celebration of island flavours.

It's great to use any leftover or stale bread for this, whether it is baguettes (typically used), a sliced white loaf, croissants or brioche. Cut into generous portions, the pudding can be served warm or cold.

RUM-SOAKED RAISIN BREAD PUDDING
POUDINE, MADAGASCAR

50g raisins
75ml golden/spiced or dark rum
500g stale, day-old baguette,
    broken into pieces
850ml whole milk
60g light muscovado sugar
3 eggs
100g unsalted butter, melted

1 vanilla pod, split lengthways
    and seeds scraped out, or
    1 tsp vanilla extract
Zest of 1 orange

For the caramel:
150g caster sugar

SERVES:
8–10
PREP:
40 MINUTES
COOK:
1½ HOURS

· Place the raisins and rum in a small bowl. Leave to stand for 15 minutes: the raisins will plump up as they absorb the alcohol.

· Place the bread pieces in a large mixing bowl and cover with the milk. Leave the bread to soak in the milk for 5 minutes, then use your hands to squeeze and squelch the bread to mash it all up.

· In a small bowl, whisk the muscovado sugar and eggs together until they are a pale brown colour.

· Pour the egg and sugar mixture into the soaked bread and add the melted butter, vanilla, orange zest and rum-soaked raisins and their leftover liquid. Beat well with a wooden spoon until combined. Let this stand for 20 minutes to soak up the flavours.

· Preheat the oven to 180°C/Fan 160°C/Gas 4.

· Next make the caramel. Place a medium pan over a medium heat. Scatter in the caster sugar and 2 tablespoons water. After a few minutes the sugar will start to dissolve around the edges. It's important not to stir the sugar as it may crystallise. Swirl the pan for even melting. Once the sugar has melted, increase the heat to medium-high.

- Continue to cook the sugar, gently swirling the pan to encourage even colouring – it should start to go a golden brown colour. At this point take it off the heat and pour it into the bottom of a baking dish around 24cm in diameter (be careful as the caramel is very hot and it may spit). Gently swirl your dish to make sure the caramel spreads evenly on the bottom.

- Using a spatula, place the bread mixture on top of the caramel and spread all the way to the edges of the dish, smoothing the top.

- Bake in the oven for 1 hour 30 minutes, or until a skewer inserted into the bread pudding comes out clean. Cover with foil if it starts to brown too quickly.

- Remove from the oven and leave to cool slightly. Run a knife around the sides of the dish to carefully detach the pudding. Place an upside down plate or large serving board on the pudding dish and invert it. Carefully remove the pudding dish – the layer of caramel will be on the top. Cut into portions to serve.

I first made this cake for one of my supper clubs at home and it was the dish that everyone kept talking about. It's the sticky rich pineapple coated in rum caramel that makes it so special.

My cousin Priya, an avid baker, lives in Central Flacq on the east coast of Mauritius. Her kitchen is always coated in a fine dusting of flour and sugar from her long hours experimenting with creative combinations and enticing bakes. On the land behind her home grows sugar cane and a little further down there is a vast pineapple field. These fruits are grown in the ground, tufts of spiky leaves reaching to the sky and, nestled amongst them, golden pineapples with juicy sweet flesh, ready to be plucked.

Priya would make upside-down cakes to use up any leftover pineapple or fruit and this recipe is inspired by her. Here I have used Mauritian Chamarel rum as it's one of my favourites, but you can use any golden/spiced or dark rum.

PINEAPPLE UPSIDE-DOWN CAKE WITH CARDAMOM CREAM
MAURITIUS

For the cardamom clotted cream:
227g tub clotted cream
1 tsp ground cardamom
   (or seeds from approx. 20 pods,
   ground with a pestle and mortar)
1 tbsp icing sugar

For the rum caramel:
300ml whipping cream
170g caster sugar
15g unsalted butter
½ tsp salt
60ml golden/spiced or dark rum

For the cake:
150g unsalted butter, softened
150g caster sugar
2 eggs, beaten
150g self-raising flour
Pinch of salt
1 pineapple, peeled and sliced
   into 4–5 circles, hard centres
   removed, brown eyes
   cut out (*see note on p.14*)

SERVES:
4–6
PREP:
20 MINS
COOK:
1 HOUR

- First, make the cardamom clotted cream. Spoon the cream into a bowl, add the ground cardamom seeds and sugar, gently mix together, and set aside in the fridge.

- Begin the pineapple cake by making the spiced rum caramel. Bring the whipping cream to a gradual boil in a small saucepan then remove from the heat.

- Place a medium-sized, high-sided saucepan over a medium heat and add the sugar with 2 tablespoons water. Heat until the sugar has dissolved, but do not stir as it may crystallise, then increase the heat to medium-high. Keep an eye on the sugar as it starts to change colour around the edges, swirling the pan for more even caramelising. The sugar should bubble until it has turned a pale honey-coloured hue.

- At this point, take off the heat and add the hot whipping cream slowly (be careful and stand back a bit as the caramel may splutter and will be very hot!). Whisk in the butter, salt and rum until it is all fully mixed and set aside. If any caramel has hardened on the bottom of the pan, place it back on a low heat until it softens again.

- To make the cake, preheat the oven to 180°C/Fan 160°C/Gas 4. Mix the butter and sugar together until light and fluffy. Slowly beat in the eggs until incorporated, before folding in the flour and salt (don't worry if the mixture goes a little lumpy once the flour is added, this will be fine).

- Cut out a circular piece of greaseproof paper and fit inside a 20cm cake tin. Place the pineapple circles on the bottom of the tin (it's ok if there's a little overlapping). Pour over half the caramel until most of the pineapple is covered by it. Set aside the other half for serving.

- Next, using a spatula, gently spoon the cake mixture over the caramel. Using the back of the spoon, spread the mixture until you have an even covering over the pineapple caramel.

- Place in the oven and put a baking tray under the shelf your cake is on to help catch any caramel drips. Bake for around 35 minutes, then cover with foil and continue to bake for another 20 minutes. Check the cake by inserting a skewer into the centre. If it comes out clean, the cake is done. Remove from the oven and place on a wire rack to cool for 10 minutes.

- Place a plate the same size or larger over the cake tin and, wearing oven gloves, turn the whole thing upside down. Gently peel back the greaseproof paper and allow to cool slightly. Serve generous slices warm with a spoonful of the remaining caramel and some spiced clotted cream.

Pictured overleaf

MADAGASCAR

MALAGASY CUISINE IS deeply rooted in Madagascar's history as a great trading port. First settled by seafarers from Borneo, the island soon flourished because of its geography connecting East Africa with the archipelagos of the Indian Ocean. Ships from America arrived laden with sweet potato, maize, peanuts, tomatoes and lima beans. Rice (*vary*) came from Indonesia and Malaysia and it now features in almost every meal: it is even used to make a drink known as *ranovola*, where rice is toasted in a pan and then steeped in hot water, imparting a wonderful toasted flavour.

Settlers landed on the fourth largest island in the world from south-east Asia, Africa, India, China and France, bringing their cooking styles and produce with them. Plantain, yam, sugar cane and coconut flourished. *Zebu* (cattle originating from south-west Asia and giving good beef a run for its money in the flavour stakes) and pigs became the most common livestock.

But it was the cultivation of sweet vanilla orchids by French colonialists in the mid-nineteenth century that put the island on the spice route map, and today it supplies eighty per cent of the world's natural vanilla. Incredible cloves, black pepper and nutmeg were grown, along with ginger imported from Asia, and all of these quickly found a way into local kitchens. The use of these ingredients is subtle – Malagasy cooking is not overly spiced – but still amazingly flavourful. One of my favourites, *romazava*, the national dish of Madagascar, sings a song of history, geography, produce and people. It's a long-cooked stew of *zebu* meat (I use beef) served with rice and vegetables, scented with chillies and ginger.

Street food is everywhere: served from stalls known as *gargottes* and simple, open-sided restaurants called *hotelys*. The Malagasy favourite is fritters known as *mofo*, meaning bread. *Mofo gasy* is a batter of sweetened rice flour poured into greased moulds and cooked over charcoal – it is popular for breakfast with coffee (another crop introduced by the French). I love the savoury fritters best of all, especially *mofo sakay*, made by combining chopped greens, tomatoes and chillies into a batter and frying them. The crunchy balls are then dunked into red chilli paste called *sakay*, which brings a hot kick. Flaky baguettes can be found on almost every street corner, along with cream horns, croissants and mille-feuille.

Like the other islands, some of the best meals are to be found along the coast with the freshest catch. Think juicy *camarons* (Malagasy prawns), tiny oysters from Morondava, and lobsters and *langouste* (huge langoustines) simply grilled. Crab is stir-fried with rice, pork and lime to make fabulous *foza sy hena-kisoa*, one of the tastiest seafood rice dishes you will ever cook.

MADAGASCAR

Antananarivo ●

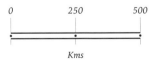

| 0 | 250 | 500 |

Kms

A classic French recipe, with my own Mauritian twist. Mangoes are grown in Mauritian villages, the countryside and can even be spotted along the roadside. The oval fruit, blushing in green and pink hues until finally yellow when ripe, hang in clusters from the trees. Here, I wanted to make a dessert that's golden and sweet, with a hint of lime, all held in a buttery, caramelised pastry. Drape over some cool yoghurt and let it slowly sink into the tart before serving.

MANGO & LIME TARTE TATIN
MAURITIUS

375g puff pastry
1 large ripe mango, peeled and sliced
  (*see note on p.14*)
Zest of 1 lime
10g unsalted butter, softened
50g caster sugar

To serve:
Zest of 1 lime
Spoonful of natural yoghurt

SERVES:
4–6
PREP:
20 MINS
COOK:
40 MINS

· Preheat the oven to 200°C/Fan 180°C/Gas 6.

· Roll out the pastry on a flat surface to a 5mm thickness. Take a 23cm ovenproof frying pan and place it the right way up on the pastry. Using a knife and keeping it vertical, run around the edge of the pan and cut out a circular shape from the pastry. Place it on a baking tray lined with greaseproof paper and pop into the fridge to chill.

· Place all the mango slices in a bowl and grate over the lime zest, giving it a good stir.

· Smear the softened butter over the base of the frying pan and scatter over the sugar so it covers the bottom of the pan. Arrange the mango slices around the pan in a fan shape until they are all lying on top of the sugar.

· Place the pan on a medium-high heat and let the mango caramelise in the sugar. It will start to bubble around the edges and go a caramel brown colour. Do not stir, but you can gently swirl the pan.

· Place the chilled puff pastry over the mango slices in the pan and gently tuck it around the sides so you can't see any of the filling (this acts as a seal). Bake in the oven for around 30 minutes or until the pastry puffs up and is golden brown.

· Take the tarte tatin out of the oven and carefully turn out onto a plate so the sticky mangoes are on the top. Grate over some lime zest and serve warm with a generous dollop of yoghurt, or just as it is.

I find the whole process of making rice pudding a joy. Watching the warm bubbling milk gently swirling around individual rice grains, with cinnamon sticks and cardamom pods bobbing on the surface – there is something soothing and nostalgic about it. It reminds me of when my mum would make it. There would be a pan on the hob, steam rising from it with the comforting aromas of cinnamon and vanilla spice. I would close my eyes and breathe in the fragrance.

My mum makes this dessert using vermicelli noodles or tapioca in the same way, and I love scooping it up straight from the pan with deep-fried breads called 'puris'. If you prefer to have it chilled, cover the surface of the rice pudding with cling film to avoid a skin forming, and place in the fridge until ready to serve.

RICE PUDDING WITH VANILLA, CINNAMON & CARDAMOM
KHEER, MAURITIUS

800ml whole milk
20g soft light brown sugar
1 vanilla pod, split lengthways
    and seeds scraped out,
    or 1 tsp vanilla extract
3 cardamom pods, seeds only,
    crushed

1 cinnamon stick
120g basmati or long-grain white rice
2 tbsp condensed milk
2 tbsp pistachios,
    crushed and finely chopped
2 tbsp flaked almonds, toasted

SERVES:
4
PREP:
10 MINS
COOK:
25 MINS

· In a large, deep saucepan, bring the milk and sugar to the boil, turn down to a simmer and add in the vanilla, cardamom and cinnamon stick. Let these infuse in the simmering milk for 5 minutes.

· Add the rice to the milk and cook over a medium-low heat for 25 minutes, stirring occasionally until the rice is cooked, creamy and has soaked up the milk. Remove the cinnamon stick towards the end. At this point stir through the condensed milk (you can add more if you like it sweeter) and spoon into small bowls. Scatter over the pistachios and toasted flaked almonds and serve warm.

Flambéed fruit in rum is the most ubiquitous dessert that you'll find in Mauritius. It's wonderfully sweet, deliciously rummy and celebrates the island's amazing tropical fruit. Normally bananas are chosen to accompany the ice cream, but I have made it here with ripe pineapple – I love the sticky juices that mingle with the rum-flavoured caramel. The interplay of hot and cold works beautifully.

COCONUT ICE CREAM WITH CARAMELISED PINEAPPLE
MAURITIUS

For the coconut ice cream:
75g freshly grated coconut
  (*see note on p.13*), or desiccated,
  unsweetened coconut
300ml double cream
200ml condensed milk
400ml tin coconut milk
1 tsp coconut essence (optional)

For the caramelised pineapple:
2 tbsp unsalted butter
120g soft light brown sugar
1 large pineapple, peeled, cored
  and cut into 2–3cm chunks
  (*see note on p.14*)
1 vanilla pod, split lengthways
  and seeds scraped out
4 tbsp golden/spiced or dark rum

To serve:
2 tbsp toasted coconut flakes/
  desiccated coconut

SERVES:
6
PREP:
20 MINS,
PLUS
OVERNIGHT
FREEZING
COOK:
25 MINS

· Place a medium frying pan over a medium heat. Sprinkle in the grated or desiccated coconut and stir for a couple of minutes until it turns light brown. Cool completely.

· To make the ice cream, whisk the double cream in a mixer or by hand until soft peaks form (this takes around 3–5 minutes). Next add the condensed milk, coconut milk and essence, if using. Whisk together until combined. It won't hold its shape, but will have quite a thick consistency. Sprinkle in all the coconut and gently fold in. Taste to see if it needs more condensed milk for sweetness (the flavour won't be as strong when frozen).

· Place the mixture in an airtight container and put it in the freezer. When it is semi-frozen, use a fork or spoon to mix it up to prevent ice crystals forming. Freeze the ice cream overnight. Alternatively, freeze/churn in an ice-cream machine.

- Once ready to serve, take the ice cream out of the freezer to soften and start the caramelised pineapple. In a large saucepan over a medium heat, combine the butter and brown sugar, stirring gently until dissolved.

- Add in the chunks of pineapple, vanilla seeds and the pod, and give it a good mix so the pineapple is mixed into the melted sugar. The sugar might clump together again, but will melt with time. Cook gently for 15–20 minutes until softened and caramelised. Remove the pan from the heat and add in the rum, ignite with a long match (be careful here, especially of your eyebrows!) and flambé until the flame goes out.

- Serve straight away on a plate with some of the caramelised sauce on top and with a dollop of coconut ice cream. Sprinkle over the toasted coconut and serve.

These yeasted breads are sweet and mellow in taste from the coconut milk, nutty with sesame seeds and sticky from honey, which is drizzled over whilst they are still warm.

The breads are of Arab–African origins and have become prominent in Comorian culture. They are normally served as a dessert with strong Arabic coffee. However, Comorians like to combine sweet and savoury and they are sometimes eaten with a vegetable curry.

SESAME COCONUT FLATBREADS
MKATRA FOUTRA, COMOROS & MAYOTTE

1 x 7g sachet fast-acting yeast
400g plain flour
1 tsp caster sugar
½ tsp sea salt
1 egg, beaten

400ml tin coconut milk
3 tbsp butter or vegetable oil
2 tbsp sesame seeds
Honey, to serve

MAKES:
10 SMALL
FLATBREADS
PREP:
15 MINS,
PLUS
1 HOUR
RESTING
COOK:
30 MINS
(EACH
FLATBREAD
COOKS IN
AROUND
6–8 MINS)

· In a large bowl, mix the yeast with 2 tablespoons warm water and leave to rest for 5 minutes. Add the flour, sugar, salt and beaten egg to the mixing bowl. Slowly pour in the coconut milk and mix well with a spatula until it is a batter-like consistency.

· Cover the bowl with cling film and leave to rest for 1 hour in a warm place.

· Once the bread mix is ready, set a medium frying pan or crêpe pan over a medium heat. Spread ½ teaspoon of the butter or oil on the base, using a piece of kitchen paper, to lubricate the pan. Once the butter has melted, scoop out 2–3 heaped tablespoons of the thick batter and plop onto the surface of the pan (it may be quite sticky). You should be able to get ten small flatbreads out of the mixture.

· Using the back of the tablespoon, make the batter into a circular shape. It doesn't matter if they are not perfectly round. For each one of the breads, sprinkle ½ teaspoon sesame seeds on the top and press lightly. Cook for 3–4 minutes per side, until it has risen to about 1cm high and is golden brown. Repeat with the remaining batter. Serve immediately, drizzled with honey or with a cup of coffee.

· These flatbreads keep for 1–2 days in an airtight container, but are best eaten fresh.

This pudding is prepared by adding roasted semolina to hot milk that has been gently flavoured with ghee (clarified butter), fennel, raisins and cinnamon. Back on the island we make this for special occasions or to celebrate religious festivals, and it is given as a kind offering to people during Hindu pilgrimages to Grand Bassin (a sacred crater lake) deep in the district of Savanne. A palm-sized amount is placed in cellophane bags and handed out. It's a really traditional recipe and my mum makes this as a snack or for tea time.

SEMOLINA GREO
HALWA, MAURITIUS

250g semolina (coarse or fine)
1 tbsp ghee, clarified butter or
  normal butter
20g raisins
1 tsp fennel seeds
1 cinnamon stick

500ml whole milk
3 tbsp caster sugar
4 cardamom pods, seeds only, crushed
½ tsp vanilla extract
2 tbsp desiccated coconut

SERVES:
6–8
PREP:
10 MINS
COOK:
UNDER
10 MINS

- In a large, dry frying pan over a medium heat, toast the semolina for 3–4 minutes until slightly darker in colour. Set aside in a bowl.

- In the same pan, add in the ghee or butter to melt and tip in the raisins, fennel seeds and cinnamon stick. Cook for 30 seconds to release the oils from the spices and plump up the raisins.

- Add in the milk, then the sugar, cardamom and vanilla. Stir until the sugar has dissolved; while the milk warms the spices will infuse. Remove the cinnamon stick and discard.

- Tip in the toasted semolina, stirring until it has soaked up the milk, making sure there are no large lumps. Take off the heat, let it cool slightly and roll into small balls or serve small portions in bowls. Sprinkle over coconut and serve warm with a cup of tea.

On Réunion is a legendary chocolate producer, Mascarin, whose range includes earthy notes of 'Bourbon pointu', the island's renowned coffee, as well as tamarind, lychee, guava and, my favourite, cardamom. Before leaving the island I stock up my suitcase with enough chocolate to satisfy the cravings.

This dessert is my ode to that chocolate bar: the deep, velvety chocolate is infused with a touch of beautiful aromatic spice. The crushed green pistachios over the top add a welcome crunch to the soft mousse below.

CARDAMOM CHOCOLATE MOUSSE WITH PISTACHIOS
RÉUNION

7 cardamom pods, seeds only, crushed
150g good-quality dark chocolate
   (minimum 70% solids), chopped
Pinch of salt
20g unsalted butter

½ tsp vanilla extract
5 large eggs, separated
3 tbsp caster sugar
20g pistachios, finely chopped

SERVES:
4–6
PREP:
30 MINS,
PLUS
2–3 HOURS
IN THE
FRIDGE
TO SET

- Lightly toast the cardamom seeds in a small frying pan for 20–30 seconds. Using a pestle and mortar, bash the toasted seeds to a fine powder.

- Place the chocolate, pinch of salt and butter in a heatproof bowl over a pan of simmering water (do not let the bowl touch the water). Once melted, remove from the heat. Sprinkle in the ground cardamom and vanilla, stir gently and set aside to cool.

- Place the egg yolks and 1 tablespoon of the sugar in a large bowl and beat with a whisk or electric beaters until the mixture is pale, thick and doubled in size. Fold in the cooled chocolate.

- In a separate bowl, whisk the egg whites to stiff peaks. Beat in the remaining 2 tablespoons of sugar until glossy. Briskly fold a third of the egg whites into the chocolate mix until fully incorporated. Then very carefully fold in the remaining whites, retaining as much air as possible.

- Pour into serving glasses or bowls and refrigerate for 2–3 hours. Scatter over the chopped pistachios and serve.

The 'tourte' is a French-Rodriguan recipe with a jam-like, tropical fruit filling encased in a buttery shortcrust pastry. These decorative pies are a real feature of the bustling Port Mathurin bazaar on the north coast of the island. They are all creatively crimped, and traditionally the names of the fruit within are written in pastry on the top of each pie. A slice of this is great as an afternoon treat or dessert. There are a few variations with the fillings and my other favourites include plain coconut, local honey and lemons, and coconut with chocolate.

PAPAYA & COCONUT PIE
TOURTE RODRIGUAISE, RODRIGUES

For the pastry:
250g plain flour, plus extra for rolling
125g unsalted butter, cold,
  cut into cubes
½ tsp ground cinnamon
1 large egg (at room temperature),
  beaten
1–2 tbsp milk
Egg or milk, for glazing

For the filling:
2 ripe papayas (or 1 pineapple)
150g unrefined sugar or cane sugar
1 small coconut, freshly grated
  (*see note on p.13*)
1 tsp vanilla extract

SERVES:
8
PREP:
10 MINS,
PLUS
30 MINS
CHILLING
COOK:
40 MINS,
PLUS
15 MINS
COOLING

· Sift the flour into a large mixing bowl and add the cubes of butter, using your fingers and thumb to rub it into the flour until you end up with a crumb-like texture. Sprinkle in the cinnamon.

· Add the egg and milk into the mixture and work together gently until you have pastry. Don't work the dough too much at this stage. Flour your work surface and place the dough on top. Pat it into a flat round, flour it lightly, wrap it in cling film and put it into the fridge to rest for at least half an hour.

· Prepare the filling by peeling the papayas. Remove the seeds, cut into cubes and place the fruit in a heavy saucepan. (Or chop your pineapple into small chunks; see note on p.14.)

· Add the sugar and cook until the mixture browns and thickens. Tip in the grated coconut and vanilla extract and combine well. Remove from the heat and allow to cool.

· Preheat the oven to 180°C/Fan 160°C/Gas 4 (see note opposite).

- Divide the pastry in two and roll out one half on a lightly floured surface, about 5mm in thickness. Use to line a 20cm loose-bottomed tart tin, pressing down to stick at the edges and trim the excess.

- Spoon the cooled filling into the tart and spread evenly. Roll out a 20cm circular lid from the remaining pastry and use it to cover the filling, pinching the edges to seal, then trim the excess.

- Decorate the pie with the remaining dough trimmings and brush the top with egg or milk. Bake in the preheated oven for 30–40 minutes until the crust turns golden brown in colour. Cool in the tin for 15 minutes before lifting out. Allow to cool to room temperature, then slice to serve.

Note

- If using a conventional oven (not fan), place the pie on the bottom shelf of the oven to ensure the pastry is cooked throughout.

DRINKS

Vanilla Chia Milkshake
ALOUDA, MAURITIUS

Watermelon, Coconut & Lime Juice
KARAA FANI, MALDIVES

Lychee, Rum & Lime Ti Punch
MAURITIUS

Tamarind Lemonade with Honey
RODRIGUES

Cardamom Chai
ALL ISLANDS

DRINKS

MAURITIUS, RÉUNION AND the Seychelles are known for their rum production, having mastered the art of sugar cane juice fermentation. Today there are many rum distillery plants that pride themselves on producing unique blends of island rums. These rich, spice-scented, dark molasses rums are actually quite potent – more than you might realise. *Rhum arrangé* is always offered after a meal in Réunion, and this flavoured or infused rum is made by adding spices like vanilla pods, cinnamon bark or slivers of fresh ginger to bottles and mixing with slices of tropical fruit such as pineapple or mango, or even aromatic herbs such as lemongrass. The bottles are then left to steep and macerate, resulting in the most enticing flavour combinations.

They can be drunk as they are (if you're strong enough!) or used to make cocktails – one of my favourites is a Lychee, rum & lime ti punch (p.241). I tend to use a good-quality dark or golden/spiced rum and, in true Creole spirit, these drinks go perfectly with any of the recipes in the Snacks & street food chapter (pp.140–179).

The fresh, reviving Watermelon, coconut & lime juice (p.238) and the Tamarind lemonade with honey (p.242) make use of the glorious fruits grown in this part of the world, creating uplifting drinks that are perfect for starting off the day or lounging in the sunshine. One of my favourite childhood treats in Mauritius was *alouda* (p.237). This milkshake-style drink flavoured with vanilla, strawberry or almond and pops of basil seeds takes me back to being that giggling, excited little girl, and today my daughter enjoys it just as much too. And finally, at the end of the day after your evening meal or when you crave a cup of something warm and soothing, a simple Cardamom chai (p.243) is all you need. My mum would make this with vanilla tea from Bois Cheri (the largest tea plantation on the island) for an authentic taste of Mauritius, but you can achieve a very similar taste with regular black tea.

My favourite 'alouda' seller is found in Central Flacq market on the east coast of Mauritius. At a corner stall, thirsty crowds huddle while sellers call out for the next order. Two large glass containers are filled with a milky liquid – one pale pink, the other a pale yellow. Inside you can glimpse the swollen black basil seeds and pieces of jelly swirling in the mixture. This is a sweet Mauritian-style milkshake with the essence of fragrant vanilla and rosewater, ladled into serving glasses, sometimes a scoop of ice cream added for extra indulgence.

To make this at home, I have used gelatine powder and chia seeds, found in most supermarkets. If you're not keen on the texture, it's fine simply to omit the jelly and seeds or add less. You can make this 24 hours ahead, but it's best to keep the jelly, seeds and milk in separate containers, and to mix them together immediately before serving.

VANILLA CHIA MILKSHAKE
ALOUDA, MAURITIUS

1 x 12g packet gelatine powder
  or agar agar
¼–½ tsp rosewater
1 tbsp chia seeds or basil seeds
500ml cold milk

1 tsp vanilla extract
2 tsp caster sugar

To serve:
Crushed ice
Vanilla ice cream

MAKES:
2 LARGE
OR 4 SMALL
GLASSES

PREP:
20 MINS,
PLUS
1 HOUR
FOR SETTING
THE JELLY
AND FOR
THE CHIA
SEEDS TO
SWELL

· Place the serving glasses in the fridge to chill.

· To prepare the jelly, place 200ml hot water in a small bowl, add in the sachet of gelatine and stir briskly until all the powder has dissolved. If it hasn't, place the bowl over a saucepan with water on a gentle boil until it has dissolved. Allow to cool slightly and stir in the rosewater. Cover and place in the fridge to set (this takes up to an hour). Once set, chop the jelly into small cubes and set aside.

· To prepare the chia or basil seeds, put the seeds in a cup with 4 tablespoons cold water. Set aside to plump up.

· To make the *alouda*, in a large mixing bowl or jug add the milk, 250ml water, vanilla extract and sugar and whisk together well. Pour the sweetened milk into the chilled serving glasses, up to two-thirds full. Add a tablespoon of soaked chia seeds and jelly pieces to each glass if you are making four and stir well. If you are making two large glasses, divide the chia seeds and jelly evenly between both glasses (around 2 tablespoons each). Top with crushed ice, or ice cream if you want a bit more creaminess. Stick a straw in each glass. You can also serve with a teaspoon to scoop up the jelly pieces.

This refreshing, gorgeously bright juice is used to break the fast for Ramadan in the Maldives. These islands have an atoll called Thoddoo that is dedicated to growing watermelons just for this occasion – they take one to two months to farm before being distributed to markets to be sold by weight. Maldivians love to add small chunks of the fruit to their juice and eat the pieces with a spoon. In my version I have blended everything into a smooth juice with coconut water and lime, which add delicious notes of sweetness and citrus.

WATERMELON, COCONUT & LIME JUICE
KARAA FANI, MALDIVES

1 large watermelon (700g flesh)
300ml coconut water
Juice of 1 lime
1–2 tbsp white sugar (optional)

To serve:
Mint leaves
Handful of ice cubes

SERVES:
3–4
PREP:
20 MINS

- Lay the watermelon on a chopping board and trim both ends with a sharp (or serrated) knife. Stand up the watermelon and slice down the middle to create two big halves. Lay each half flesh side-down and cut in half again. You'll have a total of four long pieces.

- Turn each quartered piece horizontally, run the knife between the flesh and the skin and slice into 3cm thick triangles. Using a spoon, scoop out any seeds and discard. Put the watermelon into a blender.

- Blend the watermelon until completely pulverised; this should only take a minute. Pour in the coconut water and squeeze in the lime juice. You can also add sugar here if you wish.

- Strain through a fine sieve into a serving jug. Add mint leaves and ice cubes and stir to combine. Serve immediately.

My Uncle Sooresh has a sprawling lychee tree in his back garden, with huddles of the pinkish-red fruit within its thick foliage. Peeling back the skin of the lychee reveals a soft, jelly-like white flesh, which has a delicate, citrussy flavour with a hint of rosewater.

I love using the golden sugar cane rums from Mauritius in cocktails. Sometimes they have a hint of spice that goes so well combined with lychees to make this drink. Just be warned that in true island style, it's very strong! You can dilute the cocktail by adding carton lychee juice, which can be found in most supermarkets.

LYCHEE, RUM & LIME TI PUNCH
MAURITIUS

8 mint leaves
1 can lychees, drained, or 425g
   fresh lychees, peeled and stones
   removed, 2 set aside for serving
2 tbsp cane syrup or brown sugar
Juice of 1 lime
150ml good-quality golden/
   spiced rum

To serve:
Mint leaves
Lime slices
Ice cubes

MAKES:
2 SHORT
COCKTAILS
PREP:
15 MINS
(IF PREPARING
FRESH
LYCHEES)

- Place 2 short glasses in the fridge to chill.

- In a large jar or jug, muddle the fresh mint leaves, lychees, cane syrup or brown sugar and lime juice, pressing together until well mixed and the sugar, if using, has dissolved.

- Pour in the rum and give it a good swirl. Strain into the chilled glasses, place one pitted lychee into each glass and garnish with mint and a slice of lime. Top up with ice cubes and serve.

The lemons grown on the island of Rodrigues are green and slightly smaller than a lime, and are mainly preserved and used to make candied treats or incorporated into spicy pastes like the Green chilli paste with lemon (p.197). I tried them in an invigorating lemonade sold at the market, sweetened with local organic honey made from eucalyptus flowers. The tartness of the tamarind adds a smooth sourness that balances this drink so it's not overly sweet.

Eucalyptus honey can be bought in some supermarkets; if you can't source it, any runny honey will do. You can find tamarind paste in supermarkets, or concentrated tamarind pulp or fresh pods are sold in Asian supermarkets and online.

TAMARIND LEMONADE WITH HONEY
RODRIGUES

50g or 2 tbsp tamarind paste or pulp
  (*see note on p.20*)
Juice of 2 lemons
3 tbsp honey, ideally eucalyptus
10 mint leaves

To serve:
Ice cubes
1 lemon, cut into slices
Mint sprigs
Honey

SERVES:
4
PREP:
20 MINS,
PLUS
2–3 HOURS
CHILLING
(OPTIONAL)

· Using your hands, really mash the tamarind pulp and try to break up the paste. Pour the liquid into a jug or mixing bowl through a fine-mesh sieve, discarding the seeds and fibres.

· Add in the lemon juice and eucalyptus honey and whisk lightly to dissolve the honey into the juice.

· Place the mint leaves in a tea towel and bruise with a rolling pin, then add to the mixture. Top up with 1 litre cold water and stir well.

· Chill in the fridge for 2–3 hours to let the flavours mingle, or serve straight away over ice cubes, a slice of lemon and garnished with mint. More honey can be added to taste.

Variation

· You can experiment with the flavour by adding slivers of ginger, cinnamon sticks or even vanilla.

Countless times I've watched my mum make chai in a small steel pot on the stove, simmering the tea until the kitchen is filled with a cloud of cardamom and cinnamon steam. She ladles it into small glasses and often serves it alongside some Semolina greo (p.226) for an afternoon treat. It's also a tradition at my dad's family home in Ecroignard on the east coast of Mauritius to welcome every guest with a cup of chai upon arrival, something that relaxes you instantly and makes you feel at home.

CARDAMOM CHAI
ALL ISLANDS

10 cardamom pods, crushed
1 cinnamon stick
½ tsp fennel seeds
1 vanilla pod, split lengthways

3 tsp loose black tea or 3 teabags
250ml whole milk
2 tsp caster sugar, or to taste

SERVES:
4
PREP:
5 MINS
COOK:
UNDER
10 MINS

· Add 600ml water to a medium saucepan, bring up to a steady boil and add in the crushed cardamom pods, cinnamon stick, fennel seeds and vanilla. Pop in the tea leaves or bags and turn down to a simmer for 5 minutes on the hob.

· The chai will begin to smell sweet and aromatic. Add the milk and sugar and gently mix to dissolve.

· Turn off the heat and leave to steep for a couple of minutes. Strain into tea cups and serve.

PLANNING A MEAL

The traditional Indian Ocean island dinner table boasts a wide array of dishes. Large bowls of robust curries or stews and platters of grilled fish will jostle for space with sautéed vegetables, bright salads and comforting dhals. There will also be a few chutneys or pickles amongst all the dishes, to offer a note of spice and piquancy. On occasion there might be a small bowl of soup with 'bredes' (greens) or fish to refresh the palate in between courses. And mounds of rice or flatbreads such as 'chapatis', 'rotis' or shallow-fried 'puri' will be passed around, completing the meal.

The menus below will serve 4 to 6 people, unless otherwise indicated.

SEYCHELLOIS MENU

Steamed Clams in Tomato Broth, BOUILLON TEC TEC (P.70)
Curry Leaf Bread Rolls (P.137)
—
Ginger & Herb Grilled Red Snapper (P.81)
Creole Saffran Rice (P.131)
—
Sweet Potato with Nutmeg & Cinnamon, LADOB (P.207)

RÉUNIONESE MENU

Pork Dumplings with Soy Ginger Dip, BOUCHONS (P.170)
—
Sausages in Spicy Tomato Sauce, ROUGAILLE SAUCISSE (P.54)
Creamy Lentils with Thyme & Turmeric (P.124)
—
Cardamom Chocolate Mousse with Pistachios (P.229)
(rhum arrangé, to drink)

MAURITIAN MENU

Chilli Dhal Fritters, GATEAUX PIMENTS (P.156)
Chilli Prawn Fritters, CREVETTES CROUSTILLANTES (P.173)
Fresh Coconut, Mint & Tamarind Chutney, SATINI COCO (P.189)
—
Chicken in Yoghurt & Saffron Sauce, KALIA DE POULET (P.34)
Island-style Rotis (P.138)
Okra & Tomato Salad with Red Onion, LALO SALADE (P.106)
—
Pineapple Upside-down Cake with Cardamom Cream (P.212)
Lychee, Rum & Lime Ti Punch (P.241)

MALDIVIAN MENU

Golden Egg & White Cabbage Pastries, BIS KEEMIYA (P.150)
—
Fish Soup with Chilli & Lime, GARUDHIYA (P.69)
Maldivian Tuna Curry, DHON RIHA (P.78)
Island-style Rotis (P.138)
(chillies, lime wedges, onions, shredded coconut on the side)
—
Banana Fritters with Rosewater, DHONKEYO KAJURU (P.208)

MALAGASY/COMORIAN & MAHORAN MENU

Chicken Wings with Tomatoes, MBAWA YA TOMATI (P.37)
—
Beef & Pork Stew with Spring Greens, ROMAZAVA (P.43)
Malagasy Coconut Rice, VARY AMIN'NY VOANIO (P.128)
Hot Chilli Dipping Sauce, SAKAY (P.196)
—
Rum-soaked Raisin Bread Pudding, POUDINE (P.210)

RODRIGUAISE MENU

Creole Octopus Salad, SALADE OURITE (P.89)
—
Pork Loin Glazed with Honey & Thyme (P.63)
(serve with mashed potato, steamed vegetables or rice)
—
Papaya & Coconut Pie, TOURTE RODRIGUAISE (P.230)
Tamarind Lemonade with Honey (P.242)

VEGETARIAN MENU

Golden Egg & White Cabbage Pastries, BIS KEEMIYA (P.150)
Potato & Pea Samosas (P.146)
Coriander Green Chilli Chutney, SATINI COTOMILI (P.190)
—

Kidney Bean, Butternut & Potato Stew, LA DAUBE (P.126)
Okra & Tomato Salad with Red Onion, LALO SALADE (P.106)
Pumpkin & Chou Chou Gratin, GRATIN DE CHOU CHOU (P.120)
—

Sesame Coconut Flatbreads, MKATRA FOUTRA (P.225)

VEGAN MENU

Spicy Bread Fritters with Chilli & Tomato, MOFO SAKAY (P.145)
Creamy Sweet Potato Soup (P.116)
—

Seychellois Aubergine & Chickpea Cari (P.119)
Watercress & Pak Choi Broth, BOUILLON CRESSON (P.115)
Malagasy Coconut Rice, VARY AMIN'NY VOANIO (P.128)
—

Sweet Potato with Nutmeg & Cinnamon, LADOB (P.207)

GLUTEN-FREE MENU

Roasted Peppers Stuffed with Sardines & Chilli, PIMENT FARCI (P.163)
—

Tilapia with Watercress & Tomato Sauce, TRONDRO GASY (P.73)
Creole Saffran Rice (P.131)
Hot Chilli Dipping Sauce, SAKAY (P.196)
—

Cardamom Chocolate Mousse with Pistachios (P.229)
Watermelon, Coconut & Lime Juice, KARAA FANI (P.238)

DAIRY-FREE MENU

Tuna & Coconut Flatbreads, MASROSHI (P.174)
—

Coconut Chicken, AKOHO SY VOANIO (P.33)
Toasted Coconut, Mango & Carrot Salad (P.110)
Island-style Rotis (P.138)
—

Tropical Fruit Salad with Vanilla Syrup, SALADY VOANKAZO (P.204)

BARBECUE/SHARING MENU

Four-spice Pork Kebabs with Peppers, BROCHETTES DE PORC (P.59)
Grilled Spiced Lamb Chops with Lemon (P.60)
Grilled Beef Skewers with Peanut Sauce, MASIKITA (P.164)

—

Toasted Coconut, Mango & Carrot Salad (P.110)
Tamarind Pineapple Chilli Salt Salad (P.105)
Curry Leaf Bread Rolls (P.137)
Creole Saffran Rice (P.131)
Lemon Chilli Pickle, LASARY (P.185)

—

Coconut Ice Cream with Caramelised Pineapple (P.222)

DOWN TO THE BEACH/PICNIC MENU

(SERVES 10)

Cumin & Lentil Flatbreads, DHAL PURI (P.158)
Green Bean, Cabbage & Carrot Mustard Pickle, ACHARD DES LÉGUMES (P.186)
Chilli Dhal Fritters, GATEAUX PIMENTS (P.156)
Coriander Green Chilli Chutney, SATINI COTOMILI (P.190)
Mustard- & Turmeric-marinated Tuna, VINDAYE POISSON (P.82)
Curry Leaf Bread Rolls (P.137)
Spicy Lamb Patties, CATLESS (P.169)
Tamarind Pineapple Chilli Salt Salad (P.105)

SPEEDY WEEKDAY SUPPERS

Sticky Chicken with Garlic & Ginger, AKOHO MISY SAKAMALAO (P.27)
Sausages in Spicy Tomato Sauce, ROUGAILLE SAUCISSE (P.54)
Tilapia with Watercress & Tomato sauce, TRONDRO GASY (P.73)
Maldivian Tuna Curry, DHON RIHA (P.78)
Smoked Fish Salad with Peppers & Green Mango (P.97)
Creamy Sweet Potato Soup (P.116)
Braised Aubergine with Potatoes & Chilli, TOUFFÉ BRINGEL (P.123)

INDEX

ACKNOWLEDGEMENTS

Firstly I dedicate this book to my generous Mama Choo, who I would watch and help in the kitchen when I was younger. Thank you for feeding me all those sugar puris, comforting dhals and 'gateaux patate' – ultimately giving me a taste of Mauritian food at such a young age. It inspired my journey into cooking and eating soulful food. You are the best company in the kitchen, I will treasure our conversations and times we cooked together for supper clubs. Only you know how hard it was!

My close family: Dad, my sister Janita and my in-laws Teresita and Muniandy. Thank you for all your words of wisdom, those essential home-cooked takeaways and keeping my daughter entertained when I was writing the book. And all my family in Mauritius, especially Uncle Sooresh for sharing my love of food and Soodesh for going above and beyond to help.

To my all-female cast who helped me put this book together! Ariella Feiner, my literary agent, I knew when we met that you had the same vision as I did. Thank you for believing in me and for bearing with me for all those months writing that proposal. And Lisa Pendreigh, thank you for being so open-minded and for embracing my idea, you gave me the unique opportunity to create this book.

My editor, Natalie Bellos, who has ultimately made my words sing beautifully, thank you for all your support during the writing of this book and for keeping me on my toes! I think

we have made something truly special. Also to Audrey, Clare, Kitty and Kay for all your help, thank you from the bottom of my heart.

The amazing #dreamteam Yuki Sugiura, Lucy Attwater, Sarah Greeno, Valerie Berry and SongSoo Kim, for all those fun shoot days! And for making my recipes look stunning: I never imagined how beautiful it would be when it came together with the photography, styling, and Sarah's gorgeous design and illustrations. Thank you for being the best team to work with.

The dynamic trio Amanda Shipp, Becky Anderson and Jen Hampson, my Marketing and Publicity team, thank you for all your support in helping me spread the island love.

And to the powerhouse women who I am lucky enough to have in my life, who I have grown up with and those I have cooked, eaten and laughed with in the span of my career in the food industry. There's too many of you to mention, but you know who you are. You are an utter inspiration and I look up to you all, I'm proud I can call you my dearest friends.

And of course to Bloomsbury for publishing my first book. Thank you for giving me this opportunity to express myself and share with everyone the glorious cuisine from this part of the world. I can't express how happy and proud I am and look forward to the exciting adventures ahead.

To all the people I have met on my travels, who have been so welcoming, thank you for sharing your stories and most treasured recipes. I hope I have shone some light on the wonderful food from these islands.

My best friend and husband, Jason. Thank you for all your words of encouragement, motivation, love and honesty. And all those coffee trips to brainstorm and make goals! You have been my rock keeping me going and I'm forever grateful.

Finally to my funny, excitable and special daughter, Persia. You may not be old enough yet to understand what mummy is doing but I hope this will make you proud and inspire you to chase your dreams in the future. Anything is possible.

ONLINE SUPPLIERS

WWW.THEASIANCOOKSHOP.CO.UK
Fresh curry leaves, ground and whole spices

WWW.SOUSCHEF.CO.UK
Pink peppercorns and specialist ingredients

WWW.THEHIPPYSEEDCOMPANY.COM
WWW.SOUTHDEVONCHILLIFARM.CO.UK
Specialist chillies

WWW.VANILLAMART.CO.UK
Madagascan vanilla pods

WWW.TASTEMAURITIUS.COM
Cari powders and *vindaye* spice mixes

WWW.THEFISHSOCIETY.CO.UK
WWW.THECORNISHFISHMONGER.CO.UK
Prepared lobsters and crabs

BLOOMSBURY PUBLISHING
Bloomsbury Publishing Plc
50 Bedford Square, London, WC1B 3DP, UK

BLOOMSBURY, BLOOMSBURY PUBLISHING and the Diana logo are trademarks of Bloomsbury Publishing Plc

First published in Great Britain in 2019

Text © Selina Periampillai, 2019
Photographs © Yuki Sugiura, 2019
Illustrations © Sarah Greeno, 2019
Additional photography © Aviv Ben/Unsplash (pp.2–3); © Jason Periampillai (p.6); © Selina Periampillai (p.9);
© John O'Nolan/Unsplash (pp.10–11)

Selina Periampillai, Yuki Sugiura and Sarah Greeno have asserted their right under the Copyright, Designs and Patents
Act, 1988, to be identified as Author, Photographer and Illustrator respectively of this work.

A catalogue record for this book is available from the British Library.

ISBN: HB: 978-1-5266-0138-4
eBook: 978-1-5266-1248-9

10 9 8 7 6 5 4 3 2 1
Writing collaborators: Audrey Gillan, Clare Sayer
Designer: sarahgreeno.com
Photographer: Yuki Sugiura
Food Stylist: Valerie Berry
Prop Stylist: Lucy Attwater
Illustrator: Sarah Greeno
Indexer: Vanessa Bird

Printed and bound in China by C & C Offset Printing Co., Ltd

Bloomsbury Publishing Plc makes every effort to ensure that the papers used in the manufacture of our books are
natural, recyclable products made from wood grown in well-managed forests. Our manufacturing processes conform
to the environmental regulations of the country of origin.

To find out more about our authors and books visit www.bloomsbury.com and sign up for our newsletters.